Paranoia: Between Leadership and Failure

Paranoia: Between Leadership and Failure

The Revenge of Psychopathy Against the Psychiatrist

Paolo Cioni

ISBN: 1505860806
ISBN 13: 9781505860801
Library of Congress Control Number: 2014922953
CreateSpace Independent Publishing
Platform, North Charleston, SC

ACKNOWLEDGMENTS

To Marco Della Luna, a successful essayist, who, through long conversations on topics of common interest, provided me with innovative ideas and reflections of rare intelligence.

To my wife, Daniela, a great reader, who provided me with the necessary impetus to read the essential classics including Dostoevsky and Musil, the protagonists of this book.

To Claudia Milletti, a psychologist, who gave me a hand with the update to the nosography of *DSM-5*.

FOREWORD

Paranoia, from the Greek "parànoia," is a term that, even in that modern language, means "madness," from "para," meaning "outside," and "nous" meaning "mind."

Psychopathology is an important part of the psychiatric discipline because it deals with studying the nature and causes of mental disorders. It is to psychiatry what pathological anatomy is to internal medicine. It has allowed us to deal with the study of mental illnesses in a scientific way and to create the current psychiatric nosology.

Paolo Cioni studied psychopathology in depth during many years of professional practice and has the ability to explain even its most complex features in an understandable way. In this book, he deals with the topic of paranoia with agility and proposes concepts and interpretations selected by the noblest traditions of psychiatric thought. Also, since he is fond of modern neuroscience, he identifies and suggests possible neurobiological and neuropsychological correlates of this psychiatric disorder. However, what is offered as an element of public interest is the ability to rationally interpret in the light of psychopathological teaching many behaviors that each of us experiences in public and private life every day. The book is in the vein of the previous creative and unconventional work of Paolo Cioni, *Neuroschiavi* (*Neuro-Slaves*), and deserves equal success among readers because of its originality and popularity in the Italian publishing branch.

Professor Aldo Ragazzoni, MD
Neurologist, neurophysiopathologist, former president of the
Italian Society of Psychophysiology (SIPF)

PRESENTATION OF THE BOOK

"Paranoia" goes beyond the common concept of disease in the form of psychosis or disorder of personality with ideas of persecution.

In this agile work, Paolo Cioni, based on his extensive clinical experience, his neuroscientific studies, and his practice in the facilities of public assistance, introduces concepts and original perspectives on paranoia. Modern scientific tools allow penetration at the biochemical and neurophysiological levels in the disease processes and also a more refined pharmacological approach, with sometimes amazing results—although they are not completely conclusive, as described in some of the cases treated by the author.

However, Paolo Cioni's view is much broader and extends to the sphere of sociology and politics.

First of all, paranoia should also be seen in its adaptive and compensatory roles—adaptive because it allows paranoiacs, through the creation of feelings of grandeur of their roles in the world, to give significance, acceptability, and value to their own existences, compensating for a lack of self-esteem and a tendency toward low moods. However, it must also be seen in its function and capacity for social gathering. Paranoid people can become leaders and can, by communicating their sense of greatness and certainty in their delusional beliefs, infect, attract, and aggregate real ideological, political, religious, or parareligious movements. The paranoid solutions to their existential problems—which their psyches have built through the mechanisms of delusion—can be exported.

Today, the Internet is a powerful vehicle for the rapid dissemination of this sharing and for the birth of rites, affiliations, and cults around the world with the support of active, regularly updated websites and related bulletins and newsletters to members, which spread revelations, channels, and programs of action. Peculiar interest is aroused in cases where there is a combination of paranoia and political power—cases that are abundant in recent history. The paranoiac, in fact, is not always a weak, marginalized subject who is socially classified as mentally ill. There are significant cases of paranoiacs in positions of great power: kings, statesmen, and political and religious leaders. These individuals are able to force their reality and their perceptions of reality on others and to adapt their behaviors to the beliefs of their delusions.

Paranoiacs with cultural and communication skills, through the certainty with which they communicate and the great explanatory and predictive power of their ideas, together with the ability of these ideas to clearly identify and separate good from evil and to give meaning to existence and action, are often convincing to ordinary people, who usually lack the critical tools to understand the mechanisms in action and who can become easily fascinated. If a paranoid person like this also has power, things can go very far—and history shows striking outcomes in this regard. I refer to the cases described by Elias Canetti in his famous essay "Crowds and Power" but also to the phenomena of judicial collective hysteria experienced in the recent past in Italy, with a set of expectations of national purification, which, of course, have been denied in reality. This happened in the nineties, when, under the name "clean hands operation," a group of magistrates in Milan brought down the entire system of political parties under corruption charges for illegal financing.

Marco Della Luna
Lawyer, psychologist, essayist
marcodellaluna.info

INTRODUCTION: THE ESSENCE OF THE PROBLEM

What is the essence of paranoia, and what is the actual relevance of this problem for society? Are there significant changes in the prevalence of this condition in the population over the course of time?

Apart from the popular meaning, "paranoia" commonly refers to a condition that persists over time, like a character trait, and is characterized by the conviction of persecution. This condition is sometimes considered in a more specific psychiatric frame: delusion of persecution.

In the past, it was believed (e.g., by Kraepelin, the psychiatrist who introduced the term) that paranoia was not particularly common and that, in any case, it would merge together with a set of varied conditions that we will deal with below.

Paranoia is, at least today, a widespread phenomenon that varies in severity from low to high, constituting a spectrum. This phenomenon is also currently underappreciated as far as important social effects are concerned.

Consequently, the essence of paranoia lies not in the delusion of persecution—instead, it is a consequence of it—but, as the French expert Lacan brilliantly showed, in a fault of reasoning. This impairment is probably not primary but linked to emotional experiences, particularly at an early age—an affecting instability that causes feelings of worthlessness and despair, along with glimpses of greatness and power that seem reactive and comforting in relation to the former. The projection on the outside of their own experiences was actually considered a fundamental characteristic of this disorder.

Paranoiacs are characterized by a particular stiffness and social insensitivity. They care only about their own mental lives. Every external argument and comparison with others' opinions disturbs them if it is not in line with their way of thinking. From the outside, they appear to completely lack a sense of reasonableness, never proceed to mediation, and carry on in a charismatic way with unusual tenacity—and their reasons usually get broad support.

An interesting point is that the arguments they bring forward are not flawless in terms of common logic and, indeed, are immediately easily criticized. The fact that they are successful is derived solely from the unwavering strength with which they carry on, so as to hypnotize, so to speak, those they confront—even entire crowds. It is known today, as detailed in *Neuroschiavi*, that we all spend most of our lives not in a state of rationality and alertness but in a subhypnotic state, corresponding to the activation of the functional system of the central nervous system that the neuroscientist Raichle (2002) called "default mode network." In this state, we are suggestible and easily manipulated. This is an explanation for being taken in by those arguments that lack in logic but that are powerful in terms of emotional significance.

The gap between the rational consistency of the arguments and the acceptance by others is truly amazing—almost magical—and it is, perhaps, the crux of the matter. Hypnosis of the masses from charismatic sects to people subjugated by "crazy" dictators is demonstrated by a series of examples ranging from the current news to history.

Apart from the large-scale crimes committed by paranoiacs in power, even the damage caused by those at a lower social level on individual victims can be dramatic in terms of their personal safety, discrediting, and persecution.

There is actually a paradox: the alleged victims, in fact, persecute their alleged persecutors. Victims and executioners exchange roles in surprising and shocking reversals of cause and effect.

Psychiatry is known, even today, for not having the means to validate the diseases (or "disorders," as it is widely accepted to call them) with which it deals.

The evaluation that leads to the diagnosis is still largely subjective. It depends on the various existing and contrasting schools of thought and is based on interviews with the patients (both what they say and how they act) and on the impressions of the specialists (the "erlebnisse"—cognitive and emotional experiences, the information directly collected from relatives or third parties, and any documentation from various sources, mainly of a medical nature, such as medical records and certifications).

The existence of various proposals concerning operational criteria, guidelines, rating scales, and psychodiagnostic tests is still unsystematic as is the possibility of using laboratory, imaging, and psychophysiological techniques that are, to date, not sufficiently developed and standardized in the field. Paranoia represents an extreme case that should worry the community more than is now discussed and complained about.

This book will suit a reader of average knowledge and absolutely does not intend to be a complete work on the subject. It breaks away from the classic psychiatric approach and intentionally limits the historical references and the debate between schools to avoid boring the reader, focusing instead on the underlying message: that paranoiacs are more common than you might think, their impact on their communities greatly underestimated, difficult to manage in the current environment, and potentially very dangerous. They make us live uncomfortably—as they also live.

There will also be a discussion of new advances in the field of neuroscience and the proposal of some strategies to manage paranoiacs, and possibly help them.

PARANOIA: KEY WORDS

> Delusion
> Persecution
> Greatness, grandeur
> Loneliness
> Morbid feelings
> Anger
> Fear
> Impaired reasoning
> Social dangerousness
> Contrasted expertise

Some individuals exist—and they are not as rare as once believed—with a high rigidity of character that borders on absolute intransigence. They are irritable when annoyed by alleged banality (they easily become suspicious and victimlike to the point of believing they are unfairly persecuted); are focused on issues that often become the very reasons for their existence; and appear to attach too much importance on everyday topics, up to the point of delusion. They display irrepressible perseverance and high affectivity, supported by enhanced emotionality, so they are often charismatic and can easily attract followers and supporters for their causes. This is due far more to *the emotional charge that motivates them and that is transfused with ease ("spreads") on the outside rather than on the logical content that should support their arguments.*

This point about the substantial weaknesses in the arguments of these individuals was controversial in psychiatry. I remember what they taught me when I was a student. Today, the lucid, systematized delusion could be called a formidable opponent of the psychiatrist. The delusion of the paranoiac is plausible although sthenic (carried on vehemently) as opposed to the confused, fragmented, and bizarre delusion of the schizophrenic.

Aspects of contemporary society that could favor the outbreak of paranoia include:

1) Population density; and
2) Thin condo walls that amplify the noise (e.g., conversations—perhaps interpreted out of context) from neighboring apartments.

Teatime conversation or pressing reality?

- Are the paranoiacs crazy subjects who are sometimes dangerous and need to be cured?
- Or are they normal persons who, though unbearable, irritable, and nasty, have understanding and volition, and whom we should possibly defend ourselves against through the police and the judiciary system?

CHAPTER 1

CLASSIFICATION DIFFICULTIES

Fig. 1

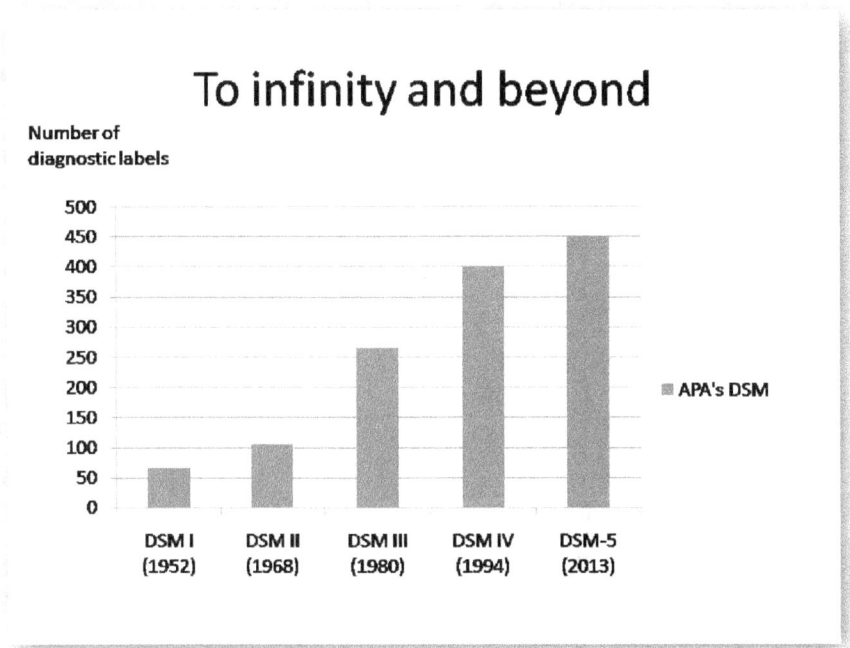

B ased on the changes in emotion, it is not so difficult to distinguish anxiety, depression, and excitement. It is also not difficult for the psychiatrist to recognize obsessive-compulsive manifestations, in which the subject complains about intrusive ideas and about having to complete rituals (washing hands, checking drawers, counting) to keep them away. Nor is it usually difficult to recognize the presence of hallucinations (e.g., auditory—hearing voices that often speak in a negative way—or kinesthetic—feeling manipulated by external forces) through the subject's "attitude of listening" to invisible speakers or the fragmented and bizarre delusions of the schizophrenics, who do not usually tend to hide them ("the Martians have gotten into the gas pipes").

It is hard, on the other hand, to fully recognize and establish good communication with paranoiacs, who feel unjustly treated as patients and are almost invariably brought to the attention of third parties. The French psychiatrist Lacan, in his famous article published in July 1931, "Semaine des Hôpitaux de Paris," expressed his strong concern that paranoia was overlooked as simply one of the many variants of personality. "So diminished, paranoia tends to be confused nowadays with the notion of character that incites, so it seems, to an inference that it could spring from the normal psychological game. *It's against this tendency that we will try to put together some reflections.* We will do this based on the purely phenomenological (analytical and scientific description of phenomena) notion of the structure of delusional states."

This downward trend on paranoia has, unfortunately, been intensified and codified by the almost ubiquitous acceptance of the classification proposals of the American Psychiatric Association (APA) with its *Diagnostic and Statistical Manual of Mental Disorders* that provides psychiatric labels that are not scientifically validated and that increase exponentially with each edition (see figure 1). The 1952 edition contained sixty-six labels. In 1994, there were four hundred, and in the fifth edition, published in 2013 in the United States and in 2014 in Italy, there were about 450.

Fig. 2

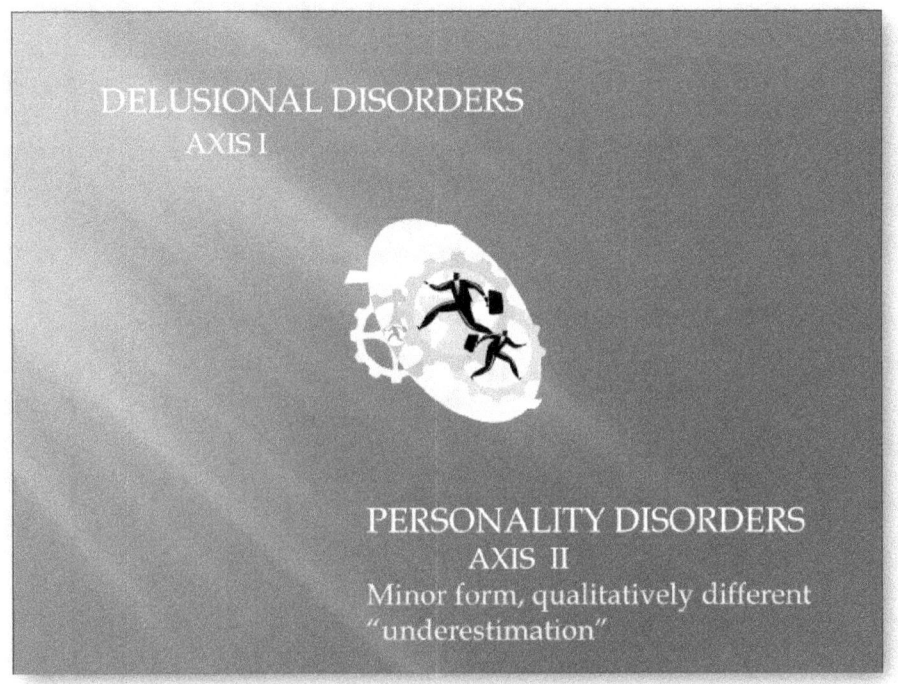

In *DSM-IV*, an arbitrary and risky separation of paranoia was made on Axis I (clinically important psychiatric disorders) using the term "delusional disorder" from another presupposed condition classified on Axis II (personality disorders, much less clinically relevant) as "paranoid personality disorder," thus meeting and justifying the worst fears of Lacan (see figure 2).

Below, the *DSM-IV* criteria for the diagnosis of "delusional disorder"(figures 3 and 4) and "paranoid personality disorder"(figure 5) are schematically reported.

Fig. 3

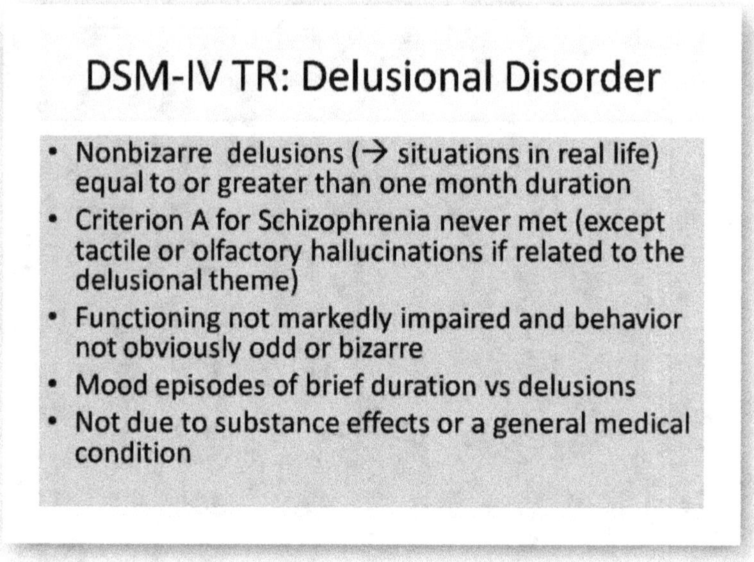

DSM-IV TR: Delusional Disorder

- Nonbizarre delusions (→ situations in real life) equal to or greater than one month duration
- Criterion A for Schizophrenia never met (except tactile or olfactory hallucinations if related to the delusional theme)
- Functioning not markedly impaired and behavior not obviously odd or bizarre
- Mood episodes of brief duration vs delusions
- Not due to substance effects or a general medical condition

Fig. 4

DSM-IV TR: Delusional themes

- Erotomanic type
- Grandiose type (greater worth, power, knowledge, identity, special relationship)
- Jealous type (unfaithful)
- Persecutory type (conviction of being malevolently treated)
- Somatic type (physical defect or illness)
- Mixed type (no one theme predominates)
- Unspecified type

Fig. 5

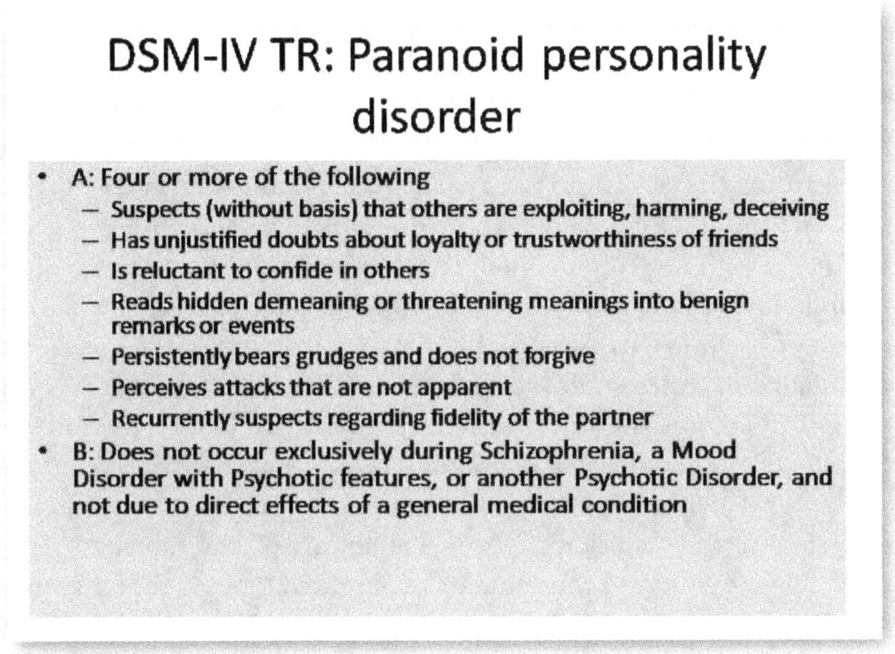

DSM-IV TR: Paranoid personality disorder

- A: Four or more of the following
  - Suspects (without basis) that others are exploiting, harming, deceiving
  - Has unjustified doubts about loyalty or trustworthiness of friends
  - Is reluctant to confide in others
  - Reads hidden demeaning or threatening meanings into benign remarks or events
  - Persistently bears grudges and does not forgive
  - Perceives attacks that are not apparent
  - Recurrently suspects regarding fidelity of the partner
- B: Does not occur exclusively during Schizophrenia, a Mood Disorder with Psychotic features, or another Psychotic Disorder, and not due to direct effects of a general medical condition

What might appear as a teatime discussion among experts is, instead, a question—just as Lacan guessed—of the utmost importance.

In practice, the distinction between a severe clinical condition and a variant of normality is based on the detection of a delusion that paranoiacs tend to be able to hide, taking into account that they do not feel "sick." With the declassified definition of "paranoid personality disorder" (see above, figure 5), the diagnostic criteria include that the subjects "suspect (without basis) that others are exploiting" them and read hidden demeaning or threatening meanings into what they say. The poor interpreter of the *DSM-IV* is not told how to distinguish this from a delusion, especially since the traditional distinction between primary (incomprehensible) and secondary or "deliroid" (resulting in affective states) delusion has been abandoned. In other words, the important diagnostic choice between a severe form and a modest alteration of character is impossible and evanescent, and it is left, in practice, to the usually benign interpretation of the interviewer.

In the new and latest edition of the *Diagnostic Manual* (*DSM-5*, APA, 2013), released in Italy in May 2014, the axes (Axis I: clinical disorders; Axis II: personality disorders, etc.) have been abandoned. Other changes regarding the classification of paranoia have also been made, further reducing the attention paid to this clinical picture.

In section III of the manual, which offers a different model of interpretation of personality disorders (despite maintaining the classification of the previous version as a matter of continuity), the paranoid personality disorder is no longer present. Out of the ten disorders in the fourth edition, only six were left. In parallel, on Axis I, the subtype "paranoid" in the subclassification of schizophrenia has been removed.

Only the delusional disorder remains, for which the criteria no longer establish that delusions must be "nonbizarre." The subtype "persecutory" is the closest to the contents of paranoid thought, but that does not absolutely capture the true extent and complexity of the condition, which is assimilated with other types of delusions, such as the somatic one. It emphasizes the delusional aspect but not the other components that characterize paranoid thought.

In addition, *DSM-5* no longer separates the delusional disorder from the shared delusional disorder. If the criteria are met for delusional disorder, then that diagnosis is given. If this diagnosis cannot be configured but there are shared beliefs, then the diagnosis of convenience is used: "other specified disorder of the schizophrenia spectrum" and "other psychotic disorder."

Basically, we do not seem to be closer to an explanation. Instead, things are now more complex. The essence of the problem is not captured, and the whole is diluted in the generic category.

CHAPTER 2

MINIMAL HISTORICAL NOTES

The first description of the disorder was reported by the famous German clinical psychiatrist Emil Kraepelin, a contemporary of Freud, who followed a different path. Kraepelin distinguished it from the two forms of psychosis he had previously identified (dementia praecox, which later became schizophrenia following the Swiss psychiatrist Bleuler, and manic-depressive insanity). In the seventh edition of his treatise of 1903, he wrote:

> *In these ones, the delusional representations form, if not the only, at least the morbid character that stands out the most. In these subjects, a delusional system tends to grow very slowly: lasting, unchanging, together with a perfect preservation of lucidity, as of the order in thought, desire, action. These forms I would like to name paranoia.*

And then, in the eighth edition of 1915:

> *Here we have the profound transformation of the overall concept of life, the displacement of the point of view with respect to the environment, which is usually denoted by the term paranoia... The importance of external circumstances in the genesis of the disease has no or minor impact. Even the unpleasant experiences [become] significant for the content of the delusion, but not for its genesis...Slow development process [is] produced by internal causes [like] degeneration [and] preparatory psychopathic traits...The root [seems to consit of] a paranoid predisposition,*

[a] mixture of huge overestimation of himself and distrust... First of all the delusion of grandeur [that can be interpreted] as a fulfillment of hidden desires and dreams...[They believe they are] Benefactors of mankind, inventors, discoverers, founders of religions, pretenders to the throne.

The following two figures (figures 6 and 7) summarize some of Kraepelin's basic concepts, as far as the differential diagnosis—DD (the distinction)—with other clinical forms is concerned.

In essence, it is believed—as the later French authors (see next chapter) develop—that paranoia is a disease that involves mainly the intellectual ability—a partial insanity or a reasoning madness—but with a strong emotional background that provides the psychic fuel to push the changes in thinking, in apparent contradiction. The other apparent contradiction of this disease of the mind is that it is accompanied by a "perfect preservation of lucidity, as of the order in thought, desire, and action." In fact, as we shall see in Lacan's theory, the intellect is actually altered at the base of the possible (but not exclusive) development of delusion.

Fig. 6

-They defend their pretensions with great force without fully losing their sense of limits
-Delusions → sense of loss → the predominant emotional tone of their excellence prevails

-DD with chronic mania (Specht): no instability, inconstancy, Irritation, inconsiderate act, changeability

Kraepelin, Emil   VIII Ed.   1915

Fig. 7

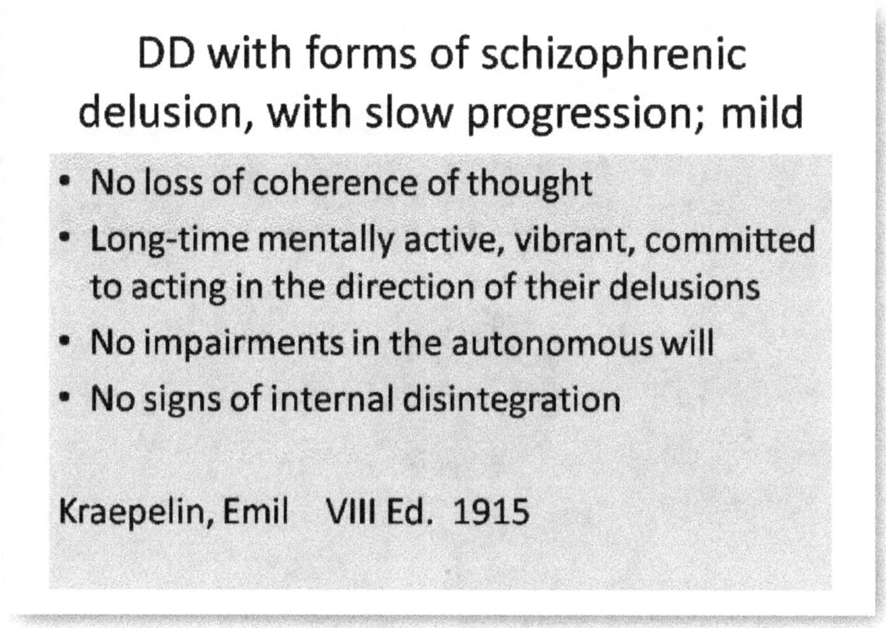

DD with forms of schizophrenic delusion, with slow progression; mild

- No loss of coherence of thought
- Long-time mentally active, vibrant, committed to acting in the direction of their delusions
- No impairments in the autonomous will
- No signs of internal disintegration

Kraepelin, Emil   VIII Ed. 1915

The French authors have their own way to confront these conditions. But we shall see later that their contribution is still the best basis for refined and coherent classification of these clinical forms, distinguishing the various conditions according to their features and behavioral consequences.

Kraeplin	French Authors
Classification and labeling	Lively descriptions of individual clinical forms
The classification is made according to the final outcome → same outcomes = same clinical label	Attention to the manifold content of delusional representations: the onset, the development of delirium, and the patient's general state of mind.

Kraepelin's Galaxy

Fig. 8

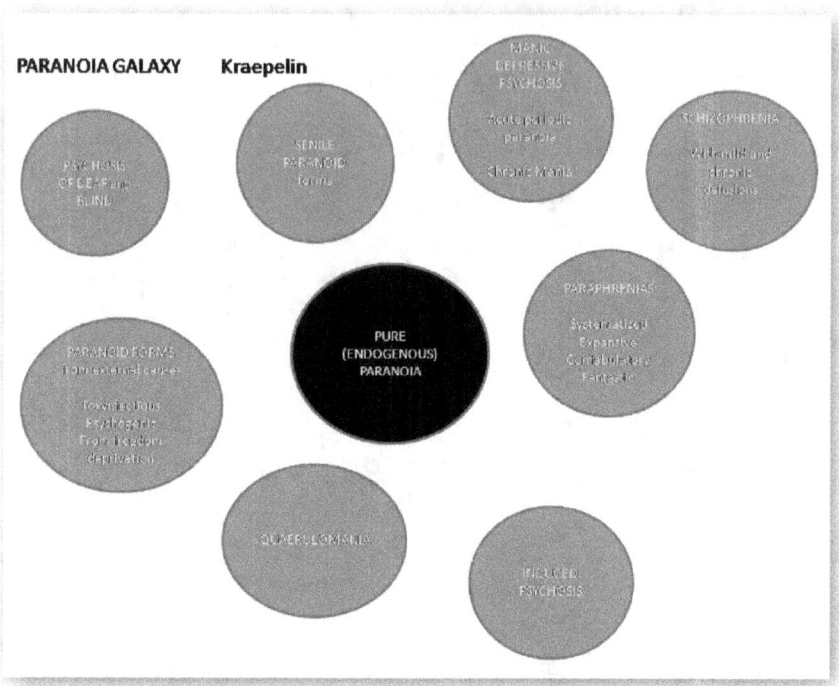

In figure 8, derived from Kraepelin's last theories on the subject, we can easily observe how varied he considered the field so as to represent a true spectrum of conditions that are different in origin and manifestation.

At the center is "pure" paranoia. On the right are the psychotic forms with paranoid features, which are close to psychoses such as schizophrenia (mild delusions with a slow course) and manic-depression (now labeled "bipolar"). Paranoia is often spoken of as "cold mania," meaning it is without acute and striking features. The so-called "paraphrenias" are transitional forms that are essentially characterized by psychotic features beyond delusions (e.g., hallucinations) but with an acceptable preservation of social functioning.

In the left part of figure 8, the "secondary" forms are reported. These include those with characteristics of reactivity with respect to triggering conditions: senile paranoid forms, dementia, and other organic forms, including Parkinson's disease and psychosis of the deaf and the blind (from sensory deprivation). When functional areas of the cerebral cortex are subjected to deafferentation, they can "discharge" autonomously, producing hallucinatory and delusional features (see Sacks, 2012, for further discussion). Secondary forms also result from specific external causes: toxinfectious, psychogenic, and deprivation of freedom (institutionalization can also produce sensory deprivation).

At the bottom of the figure, there are two other forms: querulousness (presenting as countless complaints and petitions to the authorities about alleged wrongs)—about which Kraepelin has swung in the direction of considering it a form of its own—and induced paranoia (which in *DSM-IV* is considered a shared paranoid disorder and which, incredibly, was canceled in *DSM-5*). The latter form, which deserves a separate discussion, is based on the possibility that paranoia can explode as an epidemic, with an "inducer" (the paranoiac) transposing totally and uncritically paranoid themes. It is the argument of "folie à deux" but with multiple subjects (paranoia of sects and of the masses).

CHAPTER 3

GENESIS AND FEATURES OF PARANOIA ACCORDING TO LACAN: THE VARIANTS OF THE FRENCH AUTHORS

Here's the diagram, taken from the quoted article by Lacan, which clearly divides the field (figure 9):

Fig. 9

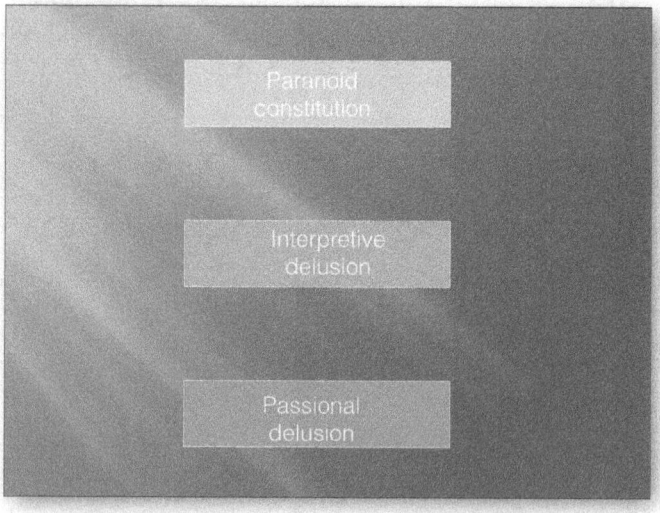

Initially therefore, there is a paranoid constitution—some basic features of the personality that may stop at that level or may form the basis of subsequent and more severe developments.

Fig. 10

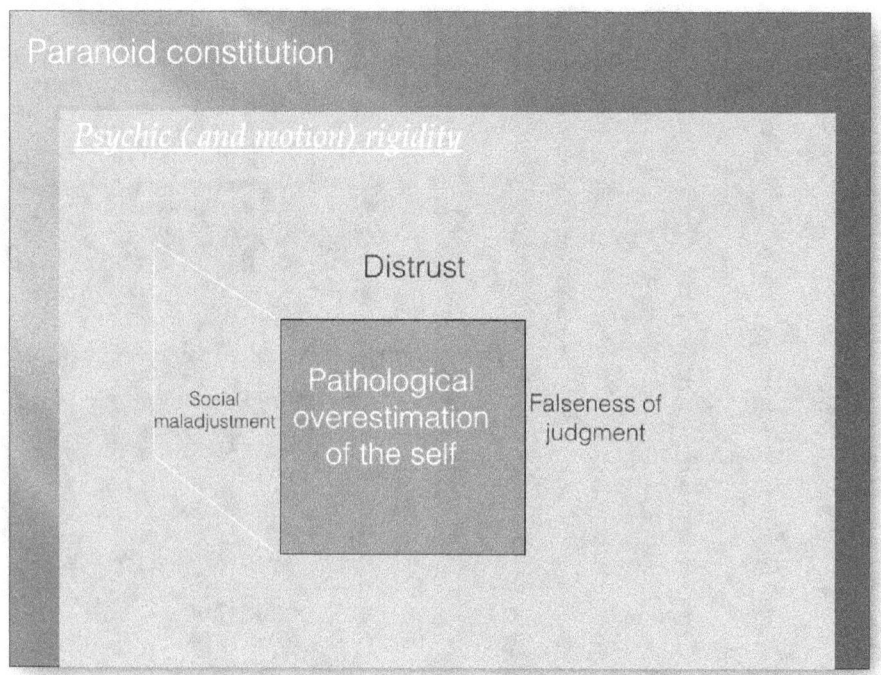

The paranoid constitution is represented by a solid with four faces (figure 10) that represent the basic dimensions.

The first face represents the pathological overestimation of the self, represented later in figure 11. It is an entirely independent characteristic in relation to the actual achievements the subject attained in life.

Here is the starting point: the expanded affective tone that subsequently conditions thought. We are confronted with subjects who experience an emotional expansion of their abilities so that they feel capable of big undertakings, committed to particular missions, and able to recognize the connections between objects and events that are usually distant and neutral elements of their lives. Note the relationship with the phase of manic excitement, from which paranoia was also named "cold mania," compared to the violence of the affective explosion in mania. As noted by Kraepelin himself, these subjects are prone to downturns in mood—probably related to preexistent gloomy feelings of inferiority and shame—and then to losing clashes with a society that does not recognize the powers they think they possess.

Fig. 11

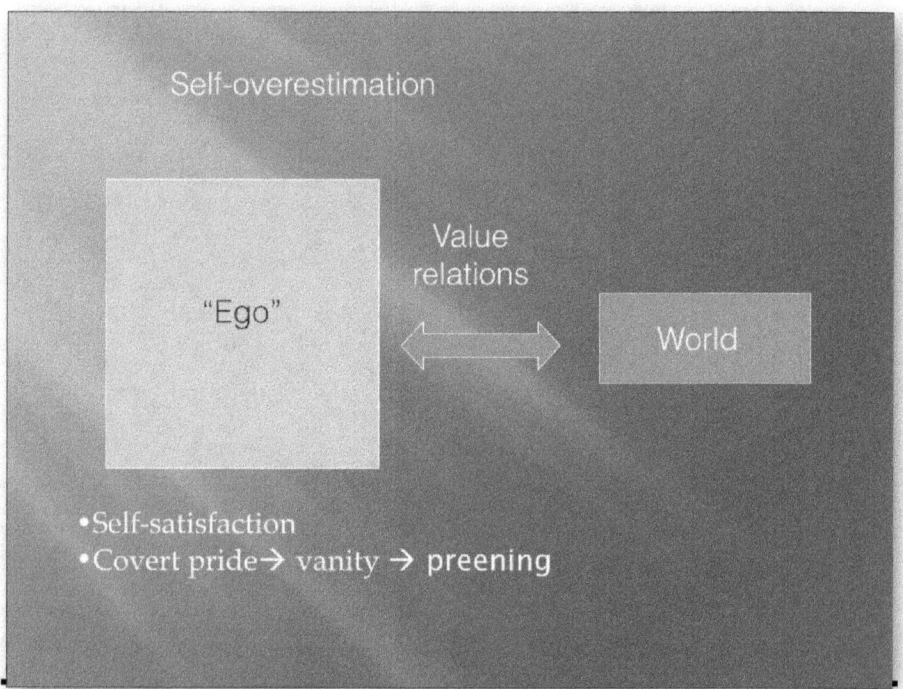

The second face represents the suspicion that imprints on the subject's actual relationships with the world. There is a fundamental doubt, which shapes the intuitions and interpretations and precipitates the emotional and anxious impulses. It is considered the negative aspect of delusion.

The third face concerns the crucial point of the disorder: the alteration of intellect (falseness of judgment). This would be a "preformed defect of classification." Because of this, judgments are channeled toward a system that is in a state of arrest rather than evolved judgment. The system takes precedence over reality, and it frames even banal, everyday life events, causing the formation of peculiar and self-reported value judgments.

Distinction between interpretive and passional delusions

Fig. 12

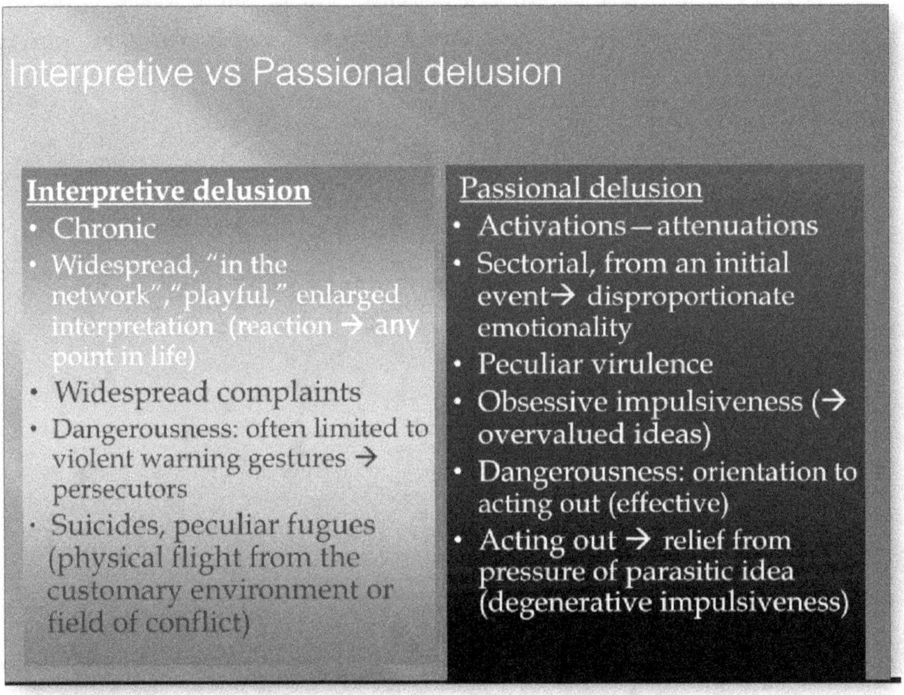

Interpretive vs Passional delusion

Interpretive delusion	Passional delusion
• Chronic	• Activations — attenuations
• Widespread, "in the network","playful," enlarged interpretation (reaction → any point in life)	• Sectorial, from an initial event→ disproportionate emotionality
• Widespread complaints	• Peculiar virulence
• Dangerousness: often limited to violent warning gestures → persecutors	• Obsessive impulsiveness (→ overvalued ideas)
• Suicides, peculiar fugues (physical flight from the customary environment or field of conflict)	• Dangerousness: orientation to acting out (effective)
	• Acting out → relief from pressure of parasitic idea (degenerative impulsiveness)

In practice, this distinction is important since paranoiacs with delusions of passion can be far more dangerous.

Delusion of interpretation (according to Sérieux and Capgras)

–   The cause of the delusion is often hidden.
–   The meaning of banal events is transformed. From primary, intuitive data and primitively unordered (experienced as obsessive ideas), a forced logic is at work (experienced as "painful, suffered").

- Neutral gestures and signals are experienced as self-referred (centripetal), leading to multiple, extensive, repeated delusional interpretations.
- The delusion is modest in its characteristics: the authors called it "of the landing, of the road, of the square." The persecutors are "modest" characters of everyday life (e.g., the neighbor, the concierge) to whom misdeeds are attributed incommensurate to their social positions.

Fig. 13

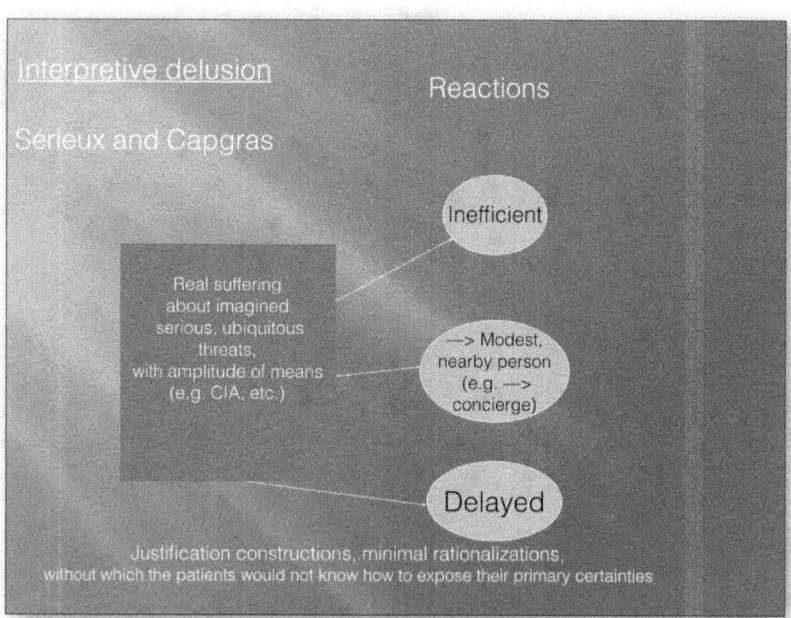

Delusions of passion (according to Clérambault)

- Delusion of claim (isolated by Sérieux and Capgras from the delusion of interpretation) or querulousness
- Erotomania
- Delusion of jealousy

Characterized by:

- Chronic hyperemotion (manic strength)
- Impulsiveness, "degeneration," amorality, perversion
- The overvalued idea is constituted by the trigger event. In psychopathology, the term "overvalued idea" indicates an ideational content with a strong affective tone, which dominates the consciousness and life of the person. The idea is not absurd or otherwise such that the person can recognize the excessiveness. It consolidates usually on the basis of impaired personalities and frequently leads to action (Poli, Cioni, 1994).
- The obsessive, impulsive urges to act out bring temporary relief and (temporary) extinction of the delusion. This pattern, however, tends to repeat and recur.

In his book *Cannibalism and Evolution* (2008), W. Lusetti theorizes that paranoia is an archaic, transnosographic (i.e., crossing the various diagnostic categories) psychic dimension that is found in:

- Schizophrenic and paranoid disorders
- Personality disorders
- Criminal psychopathies
- Affective psychotic disorders
- Neurotic and dependence disorders
- Anorexia nervosa, etc.
- Organic disorders (dementia, epilepsy, etc.)
- Sexual perversions

According to Lusetti, therefore, the predator-persecutory ideation is a basic behavioral model (basically brain software—a biological structure that can be used if necessary) that forms a pattern of antipredator behavior (together with repair and guilt) of ritualization and mastery of death. It is also the basis of religious or magic rituals, war, and idealistic reactions.

Overflow and virulence of the logical function with the formation of sophistry and paralogisms are also characteristic of this alteration of the intellect. ("Fous raisonnants" means crazy reasoners, according to Sérieux and Capgras.) Yet as we have seen, these features paradoxically give these individuals chances of success, with their appearance of rigor, the charm of "appealing" ideas, and the stubbornly unchanged statements—they back off for nothing and no one.

The fourth side is represented by social maladjustment. These subjects lack elasticity and sympathy. They are unable to build on successes to their own happiness, and they fail to submit to the disciplines (laws) established by the group, as they are always in unresolved conflict. There is ambiguity in their morals, as they are torn between the rejection of society and the need for acceptance. Real life brings cruel suffering, with hostility in social relations.

CHAPTER 4

PARANOID TYPES

Sthenic paranoiacs
> Based on the disappointment that others do not think highly enough of them, they unleash their anger, which characterizes their social reactions.

Frail paranoiacs
> Feelings of confusion and misunderstanding of reality prevail. Uncontrolled fear is unleashed, from which potentially dangerous actions spring.

Basic characteristics of paranoia:
- Social maladjustment with low afferences (loner, isolated)
- Lack of reasoning (cognitive impairment)
- Hypertrophic ego (expanded affectivity)

These features are present in varying degrees in individual paranoiacs, giving rise to different profiles, depending on the prevalence of the considered characteristics and the variable weights of each of them. The final result will be very different with respect to specific behavioral manifestations.

Fig. 14

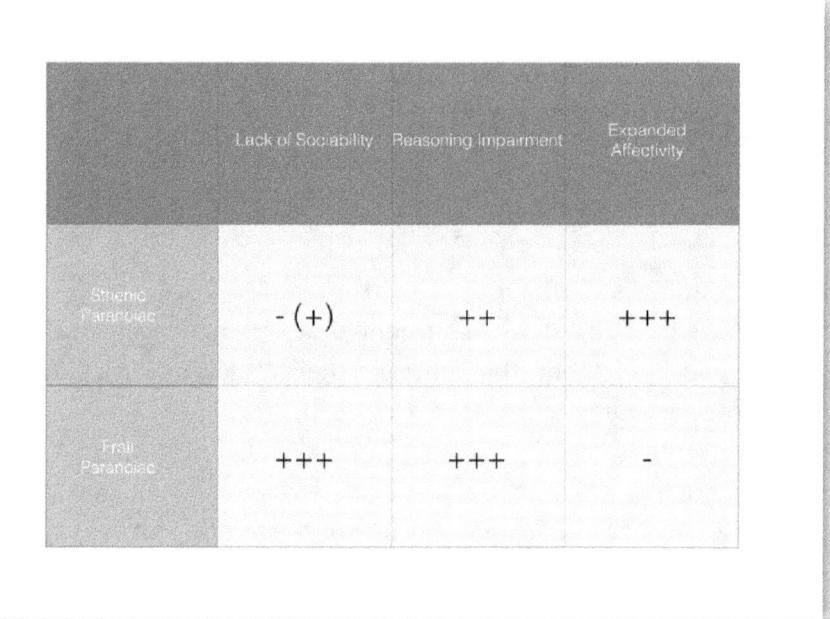

Figure 14 shows the presence and consistency of the individual characteristics for the sthenic and frail types.

It is obviously possible that we may find intermediate forms that create complex mosaics.

Sthenic paranoiacs can hold important positions in society—politicians, magistrates, and so on—that they achieve through their emotionally poignant activism (charisma) aimed at promoting their personalities. Their impairments in reasoning paradoxically help them with this achievement, as they avert instances of self-criticism and, like tanks, sweep away every obstacle that appears. They are actually executioners disguised as victims. They may have committed many acts on the border of the law or outside of it under various pretexts—which are often, incredibly, accepted, given their stubbornness and steadiness. However, when the law tries to submit the bill on the basis of absolute evidence, they assume the role of victim. They feel they are burdened by obstacles and their grandeur is misunderstood. They are the ones who want to save the country, which will be lost without them—but they are hindered by envious and bad enemies. Consequently, they display their anger in the form of wrath and indignation and are often able to raise mass movements in their favors.

The paranoid leaders try to impose their emotional and cognitive maps of reality on their environments, including contents, values, and methods. See the part devoted to the paranoid magistrate in Marco Della Luna's book *Le chiavi del potere* (*The Keys of Power*). See also Elias Canetti's book *Crowds and Power*, especially the part about the paranoid king (see below).

We should consider the possibility that the rigidity and defectiveness of paranoid thought are caused by the unadaptable and immediate needs of internal cohesion, due to a lack of structure and maturation of emotional management, where the internal need prevails on the need for external adaptation. Hyperactivity of thought takes the place of confronting reality, and, thus, the paranoiacs achieve an illusory adaptation rather than an actual adaptation to objective reality. In other words, the paranoiac makes ends meet by depending on fantasy rather than on reality. So the delusional district attorney relies on the theorem that he builds himself rather than on actual investigation, which satisfies his hunger for power less and requires more hard work.

Marco Della Luna's view is interesting in this context. He sees paranoiacs at a crossroads, with thoughts that do not correspond to reality. They may become successful leaders, and then reality is adapted to their delusions—so the delusions do not appear as such; or they do not, and then they becomes losers, sickly, or possibly criminals.

This concept is expressed in *Le chiavi del potere* (2003):

> *I would submit, curiously, as the portraits, painted by the press, of some assault investigators, justicialists, prone to abuse their powers on the person under investigation, could be used to*

represent a person whose psychic organization is of the paranoid type. This interferes in the execution of the office duties, alienating a subject from the procedural legality, without preventing the achievement of useful results in the abstract and in themselves. And the paranoid magistrate, as the paranoid monarch (see the case of Sultan Muhammad Tughlak, widely described by Elias Canetti in Masse und Macht*), and every powerful (Machthaber) paranoiac, succeeds where the common paranoid fails. He/she succeeds, therefore, to compel external reality to conform to his/her beliefs and delusional claims, so that he appears to himself and others healthy, right and ultra-powerful, while the powerless paranoiac crashes into a harsher reality of his/her delusion and is recognized as insane. The investigating magistrate with paranoid personality of this type, uses his/her own real power, exercising it often in violation of the law and the rights of the defense. He/she succeeds in having his/her delusion approved by reality, and all evil transferred to the investigated subject, forcedly. The latter was often his protégé of former times, and he is now crashed down also with the delusional support of public opinion, which, in its immaturity, identifies him/her as the bearer of a great narcissistic confidence, aggressiveness and power, while it counter-identifies with the scapegoat...He/she is not to be imprisoned since he/she is able to put the others into jail.*

The magistrate in question thus becomes...the socially most dangerous subject of all, because, in order to feel safe not to be condemned or destroyed, he/she must condemn or destroy incessantly the neighbor.

Paranoia can also be considered the opposite of empathy. The paranoiac is cold and aloof and does not pay attention to environmental feedback. They follow their own reasoning, which are not logical arguments but a series of justifications to vehemently assert their right to be important members of the community. They actually turn all around themselves. The arguments follow. They attack and are accepted by others because they vehemently spring from an overflowing, sometimes charismatic structure. For the most part, they can never be wrong because any opposing argument is not considered. This is not always true, as we have seen some paranoiacs who are not charismatic and who act in "self-defense" with respect to their perceived vulnerabilities, basic insecurities, and feelings of inferiority that may suddenly appear. They can be very dangerous.

The frail paranoiac is an entirely different affair. These individuals occupy marginal positions in society. Their lack of reasoning is due to globally underdeveloped psychic abilities (they may have lived in isolation or may be mentally challenged). Their inability to understand a complex and changing reality makes them easy prey to feelings of shame and fear, toward which they react rashly and rarely with premeditation.

Empathy is an identification with another person, rather than a mere projection. Someone with empathy is able to adapt to the reality, sensitivity, and needs of others. Empathy is the basis of social behavior, and a lack of empathy is the root cause of many antisocial behaviors.

In this regard, a reference is important to the relatively recent but well-known theory of "mirror neurons," the simulation of which is central to learning. I quote the summary from *Neuroschiavi* (*Neuro-Slaves*):

> *A group of Italian researchers at the University of Parma (Gallese and Rizzolati), initially through studies carried out on macaque monkeys, has developed one of the most interesting and credited theories on cerebral functioning (which, unfortunately, involves the usual risk beyond the intentions of the authors, evidenced in such cases of enormous cultural success, of becoming a new, all-explanatory, secular religion): the theory of mirror neurons. These researchers observed the*

activation of some prefrontal areas (premotor areas) in monkeys, not only for the performance of complex actions (e.g., grasping objects), but also in relation to the observation of the same action performed by others, or even to listening to sounds about the same action. Similar results have also been reported in humans. It seems that there are groups of neurons devoted to recognizing specific actions based on their targets—for example, taking something to eat (not just taking anything). The act would be basically the same, whether accomplished with the mind or if accomplished with a tool; so much so as it is performed by another macaque as it is completed by a human being; so much so as you look around the whole gesture as if you capture only a part.

Mirror neurons are therefore important to understanding the intentions of others, and the lack of them can determine relational difficulties and perhaps even autism, as Legrenzi and Umiltà write in their essay "Neuro-Mania" (2009). The conclusion is that when we look at someone who does something, in addition to the activation of various visual areas, there is a concomitant activation of motor circuits that are recruited when we ourselves accomplish that action...Our motor system becomes active, however, as if we were performing the same action we are seeing...To perceive an action is equivalent to simulating it internally.

Along this line of research, Avenanti et al. published an interesting article about the empathetic behaviors (shared pain) in the journal *Nature* (June 2005). Motor responses to our own pain was noted. We react by freezing or escaping. This is a significant adaptation that led to our survival.

This is a summary of their study:

- Video of a needle penetrating a hand, foot, and tomato is shown to volunteers.
- Transcranial magnetic stimulation (TMS) measures magnetic fields: evaluation of evoked potentials in the motor system (excitability).
- Similar motor responses were seen in subjects who observed pain experienced by others. Correlations were seen in the evaluation of the sensory qualities of the pain that was attributed to the model and with measurements of the sensory (but not emotional) state or trait empathy.
- Primitive, involuntary, unemotional sensory perception led to the emergence of social bonds in evolution. Archaic, observational, and imitative learning led to reacting to the pain of others.

In conclusion, when we see others (even strangers) in pain, we put ourselves in their shoes. The motor cortex reacts in the same way as if we were suffering ourselves. There was a decrease in excitability in the motor system (equal to anesthesia) in response to the viewing of needles penetrating a hand or foot but not a tomato.

This discovery may be the prelude to understanding diseases where social bonds are distorted. We can offer suggestions for therapy, such as watching someone suffer while the patient experiences pain. This may lead to the modulation of the perception of pain.

Prefrontal (ventromedial, right) malfunctioning (Damasio)

- Normal intelligence quotient (IQ)
- Bizarre social behavior
- Inability to plan and consider future consequences
- A lack or shortage of empathy, emotional involvement, embarrassment, compassion, and guilt
- Lacks the use of accumulated personal experiences to classify situations and determine whether the future outcome will be punitive or rewarding
- Caused by genetics, social, and cultural factors
- Effects are similar to cocaine, opiates, and alcohol

In *Looking for Spinoza* (2003), Damasio describes a particular malfunction of the prefrontal cortex, especially in the ventromedial right hemisphere, and, "in a less pure form," in the parietal region of the same right hemisphere, where:

> *The subject does not usually unfold the innate repertoire of emotions and social feelings. At the very least, he ends up interacting with others in an unnatural way; he reacts inappropriately to many social situations attracting, accordingly, improper*

reactions from others, and, as a result, he gets a distorted idea of the social world. Secondly, he does not acquire a repertoire of emotional responses tuned to specific previous actions: in fact, learning about the existence of a link between a particular action and its emotional consequences presupposes the integrity of the prefrontal region. In these subjects, the experience of pain, which is part of punishment, is disconnected from the action that caused the punishment itself; therefore there will be no memory of such a connection to be used in the future; the same goes for the pleasurable aspects of gratification. Thirdly, and finally, there is a lack of processing of personal knowledge about the social world. The classification of situations, the classification of—adjusted and inadequate—responses and the organization and connection of conventions and rules are distorted.

Such a defect could have many causes: from an abnormal chemical signaling with a genetic basis to social and cultural factors.

In conclusion, our learning is due to imitation/simulation of the behavior of our fellow human beings. What they did and suffered involves us, as if it happened to us. Normally, our behavior is influenced by positive or negative emotions elicited from social feedback in response to our previous behavior: *reinforcement* if positive, *extinction* if negative. There are some people who, for various reasons, are not affected by this feedback filter. They lose the ability to act empathically with the environment and demonstrate detachment, coldness, cruelty, and antisocial behavior. In paranoid individuals, it is common to find a lack of empathy, and this could be one of the focal points to work on, to: 1) create specific tests to recognize and evaluate them and 2) use targeted treatment to train them to develop it.

CHAPTER 5

CASES FROM LITERATURE

This section describes some famous paranoiacs to whom literature has given celebrity; the first two are interesting cases of paranoiacs with literacy skills, which helped them describe their disorder. The third is a frail paranoiac created by the brilliant imagination (but how distinctive and deep he is!) of the great writer Robert Musil.

1. Daniel Paul Schreber

Daniel Paul Schreber was the son of a renowned educationist known for his particularly rigid ideas. He became a magistrate and the president of the Court of Appeal of Dresden. At the age of fifty-one (1893), Schreber had a delusional crisis that became chronic. He took refuge at the psychiatric clinic in Leipzig under the care of the anatomist Flechsig. His extraordinary autobiographical *Memoirs of My Nervous Illness* was published in 1903 by the publisher Mutze in Leipzig, with the intent to "offer his person to the judgment of the experts as an object of scientific observation."

The book elicited the interest of psychiatrists. The first interpretative essay was written by Freud in 1911 in a number of issues of the *Jahrbuch Journal*. Freud made it the object of his theory on paranoia, which was based on homosexuality and projection. Many later developments, from the psychoanalysts Jung and Lacan to Canetti, brought strings to their bows through the Schreber case. Jung emphasized references to various mythological, poetic, mystical, and psychopathological materials. Lacan found inspiration for the concept he introduced as the foreclosure:

It is the fault of the Name of the Father…through the hole that opens in meaning, starts the cascade of rearrangements of the signifier, from which the growing disaster of imaginary proceeds, until that level is reached where signifier and signified stabilize in the delusional metaphor.

Canetti used it to denounce the indissoluble connection between paranoia and power. The obsession with conspiracy is equally important for the paranoiac and the powerful person.

Beyond the specific interpretative attempts, *Memoirs* itself offers interesting ideas to find the genesis of delusion and about delusional mood.

As soon as I abandon myself not to think about anything, or, which is the same thing, I interrupt an occupation witnessing the activity of the human spirit, for example in the garden I stop playing chess, immediately the wind rises…The so-called roaring [painful experience lived by the subject]. The reason lies in the fact that God, as soon as I abandon myself not to think about anything, believes he can withdraw from me as a person who would be stupid.

Schreber, on October 1, 1893, assumed the new post of president of the Court of Appeal of Dresden, but actually his life was a living hell. He was fatigued and sleepless, and he heard strange "crunches in the wall." He withdrew as sick and took a trip with his wife but felt "oppression at heart." He had thoughts of death and attempted suicide. He was hospitalized in the psychiatric hospital, but the "nervous overexcitation" got worse and worse. He was no longer able to devote himself to intellectual pursuits.

For my spiritual collapse I found decisive, in particular, a night during which I had an absolutely unusual number of pollutions (roughly half a dozen). Since then, the first symptoms of a relationship with super-sensible forces became clear, in particular of a nervous conjunction that Professor Flechsig had made with me, in the sense that he spoke with my nerves probably not being present. By this time I also had the impression that Professor Flechsig harbored no good intentions towards me.

...But in me...the case occurred that my nerves were put in motion from the outside and incessantly, without a break... The way in which this influence occurred over the years has assumed forms that were always against the Order of the World and the natural human right to freely dispose of the use of his own nerves, I would even say more and more grotesque forms. So soon enough this influence occurred in the form of a compulsion to think...The essence of the compulsion to think is so that the man is forced to think incessantly...It was limited from the outset by the rays that were in relationship with me, and that continually longed to know what I was thinking...With this senseless question [what is he thinking now?], I was soon forced to take refuge in a system of falsification of thought, giving the question above even the answer: about the Order of the World... That is my nerves were forced by the action of the rays to make those vibrations corresponding to the use of these words...Mostly dead souls were the ones who became interested in me...Which disastrous confusion would fill...my head...with a dreadfully monotonous repetition of the same phrases.

The second point that should be treated...concerns the trend in the Order of the World, toward the emasculation of a man who is in continuous contact with the rays. These relations, on the one hand, are connected with the nature of the nerves of God, thanks to which bliss (the enjoyment of it...), although not exclusively, is nevertheless, at least at the same time, an extremely intense feeling of voluptuousness.

2. Ernst Wagner

Ernst Wagner was a German primary school teacher who believed he was being persecuted for his sexual behavior in the distant past (he vented his sexual impulses on animals). Because of this, he spent a decade developing a detailed plan, which he carried out in 1913. He murdered his family (his wife and four children) to "free them from shame" and drove the inhabitants of the town where he had taught years earlier (Muelhausen) from their homes by setting fire to their barns. Armed with rifles, he also shot those he encountered. His intention was to hit only the males, whom he believed would have mocked and taunted him with allusive gossip in the village tavern, for "revenge." He claimed to have "accidentally" struck two females. Nine people were killed in addition to his entire family.

The case of Wagner is of great interest because, in addition to having been studied by the big psychiatrists of the time (the expert who judged him insane for "paranoia" was Gaupp), Wagner provided firsthand material, having written an autobiography in three parts and a drama in three acts, *Wahn (Delusion)*. In these, he reported with great depth and competence all the "internal movements" that had led him to action—he had obviously studied what specialists had written about him.

Without the need for intermediaries (to be mentioned, however, the beautiful book dedicated to the subject by Cargnello), Wagner made the character that represented him (Ludwig II of Bavaria, who fights so that his kingdom is not assimilated in the German Empire and is considered crazy) say the following:

> *There is grandeur in the stars; they run all linked to a constrictive chain. If there's magnitude above the stars who claims to know? What is madness, what is the truth: who can tell?*

Then he provides a comprehensive and absolutely illuminating framework of the various steps of the disorder:

His Majesty is suffering from delusions of persecution...Who would not think, in fact, about anything completely different, a delusion of grandeur?—Only in ideas of greatness, the sick mind seemed satiated, only in the world of grandiosity, the distraught soul seemed complacent. Well, the delusion of grandeur is present, but only as a consequent and secondary feature. Persecution and grandeur delusions mostly appear together. They are like the sound and its echo, like the object and its mirror image, like the coming and going of the pendulum. The delusion of persecution is the face and the essence; the delusion of grandeur, the mask and the appearance. This is the necessary defense of the tormented, the self-exaltation of the one who sinks, the desperate struggle for self-affirmation. Strength, the weak wants to simulate, lying to himself. His Majesty does not live in the force, but in fear. Fear is the loneliness of His Majesty, fear is misanthropy, fear is his hatred...Where is one capable of the most courageous of all statements: I fear?...The fear of the madman, however, is a crazy fear: crazy in reason, crazy in the torment, crazy in the consequences of the plan and action. His Majesty does not live in splendor, but in misery...Delusion of persecution? It is the sum of all the pains of the earth, it is hellish torment...Therein lies the disease, madness: there is no reason, no sensible reason, any reason that is obvious to the average person. But for the mentally ill, crazy imagination has the same reality of the most actual reality; constriction hovers over him. Haunting feelings burden him, and the feeling compels the thought, and the thought forces the will. And here he is in chains: chains derived from his own spirit; the one who is offering help to him becomes his executioner, who tries to free him a despot. Those who are forced to feel restless, tormented, and persecuted seek motivations, look outside themselves what instead is within them, look, look until they find...the most insignificant, the most ridiculous and the most false reason.

And, especially, the figure of the psychiatrist, who then perishes, involved in the suicide of the king, says:

The hatred, the most deadly hatred of His Majesty will hit me. Because of my expertise. Cesarean delusion, the one of Caesars— so it is called the delusion of persecution of the great—would throw me to the beasts, if we still would have that habit.

The king resumes:

The fool wonders like the criminologist: who has an interest in this? If the starting point and the direction are wrong, the reasoning continues in an even more insightful and obstinate way: no link is missing in the chain of logical deductions. Why His Majesty fears the gentlemen? Because the mentally ill of this type does not want to be peered into the very soul and fears all to whom he attributes this ability...snubs and avoids the most gifted. The disease turns the most confident expansiveness into the most closed inaccessibility. Basically, His Majesty wants to make sure everyone understands: this is my skin, what it contains must not exist for anyone. For who is believed to be spied by enemies will remain in his cave, will wrap with thorns... will show teeth and claws...Escapes are his constant changes of place, escape now to the big, big sea.

The psychiatrist resumes:

What is so feared and hated is the morbid core...He would be equally unhappy...because anyway ill...the disease that struck his mind would not be healed because of this. True, these unfortunates have a reason to fear, but of themselves they should be afraid or better of their misfortune. There is no escape.

The prince asks, "So there is no hope of recovery?"
The psychiatrist says:

> *Probably not...Psychiatry knows little, and this just is not even sure. Just because if we knew more about the law and the mechanism of the sick soul, the question of the mind would be resolved. A scientific theory is not a truth. We doctors are forced to point out the resemblance of some cases when we want to make a prognosis...His Majesty carries the weight and the curse of heredity...How much a presentiment can be awareness of the disease, it is difficult to say for those who are far away...Some strong understanding—a mentally ill does not have to be, at least for a time, a feebleminded—tends to deceive the sick; it is also understandable that self-consciousness avoids to recognize a fact that would not have another meaning but total despair.*

And then the king affirms, "The insane has the wit of ten wise people and courage as a field marshal one hundred kilometers behind the front lines."

A nurse adds, "We nurses are not afraid of patients who curse and threaten. Dangerous are not those who are grumbling, but the silent ones."

3. Moosbrugger

Moosbrugger is a character in the book by Robert Musil, *The Man Without Qualities* (1931–1942). He represents an almost pure frail paranoiac, as framed in the original classification of this book. He is, essentially, a socially isolated, mentally defective person who struggles to manage in a complex reality by implementing "reactive" aggressive behavior that is supported by fear. He still has flashes of genius.

Here is a bit of description from the book:

> *Thirty-four-year-old [carpenter] with all the signs of goodness...*
> *He had killed a woman, a prostitute, in such a gruesome way. [He was] a very lonely man [and] he had no friends. Occasionally*

the strongest instincts spilled out his personality…But maybe he was lacking education [or] the chance to become something else, an exterminating angel, an arsonist, a great anarchist.

And here, on this basis, grandeur arises:

He did not deny his misdeeds; he wanted them to be seen as unfortunate accidents of a great view of life…He avoided as long as he could, not to be provoked, but did not always succeed.

And Musil wrote a masterly description of the defect of reasoning fed by enveloping thoughts:

Especially the females were in league against him…an impostor who herself was mocking a man while enervating him and reciting the play…Certain thoughts are like strings, and twist in infinite windings around the arms and legs…He knew that he would not ever be released because he himself pulled it behind.

He is driven to action by fear, which is supported by somatic sensations:

His tongue…was as if attached with glue, gave him a painful sense of uncertainty…Pains tormented him…He stood in front of a clear boundary, and it could be said soundless…And after a while that this lasted, M was afraid.

Very interesting aspects are detailed by Musil on relations with the media professionals, legal practitioners, and health workers whom the paranoiac faced.

From such atrocities the reporters did not know how to return to the good-natured face of M…And how to renounce to the idea of the evil murderer and to transfer the incident from his own world to that of the disease...In this they agreed with psychiatrists who had constantly fluctuated in declaring him now healthy now irresponsible.

Today the essential happens in the abstract, and the irrelevant in the reality...Sometimes, however, he himself embellished it with reminiscences of sermons heard in church...And built it with the dictates of the simulation that are learned in prison... All his hatred was for the psychiatrists who believed that they could attend to his hard case with a couple of foreign words... As always...Expert reports on his mental state staggered under the pressure of the overlying conceptual legal world...to prove his superiority over psychiatrists and expose them.

CHAPTER 6

FOUR CLINICAL CASES

These real-life cases will be treated in such a way as to make them unrecognizable. They will be deliberately anecdotal to highlight the specific components of general interest and the disruptive aspects of the disorder.

1. Case "A"

A sixty-year-old former mason, long since migrated to a region far from his native land. He is retired with a primary school degree. He broke all relations with his family members, former friends, and acquaintances, especially with his wife, whom he does not want to hear about anymore. His children, a boy and a girl, occasionally continue to have some contact.

He lives in an apartment in a large building in the suburbs. He spends almost all his time at home, using two computers ("one for input and one for output"). He comes out to go to the shooting range, an activity that he grew interested in only in adulthood, practicing it in a systematic way so that he became an expert shooter.

In the apartment above his, two families left, selling at bargain prices. He accused the neighbors (especially the males) of not respecting him (for example, by not always wearing slippers and by flushing the toilet at night specifically to disturb him and taunt him). He stalked two women in the building, and they reported him to the police. He was convinced these women went to specific places to plot against him and that they were "whores." In fact, he was probably attracted to them.

He began to manufacture firecrackers at home and exploded them in the street at night. This drew protests from people in nearby condos, resulting in the collection of over forty signatures against him. It also attracted the interest of the public prosecutor, who reported him to the competent public health service and ordered an expert opinion to determine his mental status and level of danger to society.

"A" was then taken, against his will, to the public mental-health service.

The things that stood out more than anything else were his pride and feelings of superiority toward the mental-health professionals. He never missed an opportunity to criticize their behavior and was particularly disrespectful in his concerns over things such as a delay (of five minutes) in home visits or at the outpatient facility. With psychiatrists in particular, he showed an oppositional and superior attitude. He boasted of his knowledge of the philosopher Seneca by quoting his work, which demonstrated the cultural inferiority of his questioners, whom he somehow intended to dominate. His mood was variable, from moments of real depression to accentuated irritability to expansiveness with grandiose themes on his role in the world. In his opinion, he was led to major acquisitions but was hampered by enemies.

Among the enemies were almost all his acquaintances. The service itself and in particular the psychiatrist were also his sworn enemies. Once, in the waiting room, he told another patient about his desire for revenge and his intention to, sooner or later, kill the psychiatrist. The patient remained upset and told the psychiatrist.

He unshakably defended his reasons. He claimed his behavior, which had attracted a number of complaints, was only "reactive" to the harassment he suffered from various persecutors of the condo and their accomplices.

A rehabilitation program was carried out, involving his attendance at the local library in order to support him in his cultural claims. It seemed that, along with his temporary compliance with drug therapy, something positive had been unlocked, but only briefly.

On his own initiative, he began attending a club against the misdeeds of psychiatrists, and there he "enslaved" another patient who also attended. He imposed strict rules on her and actually made her become his slave. Even through the intervention of her treating psychiatrist, it was hard to take her away from him. The letter sent by the club to the mental-health service is reported below.

The expert requested by the prosecutor would not have been successful in that A had hidden his actual treating psychiatrist from the court. He contacted another public psychiatrist and, through flattery, convinced him that only he could understand A and that A was not "a bad guy" as the others believed. By chance, the court expert came into contact with the treating psychiatrist, who alerted him about the actual severity of the clinical case and gave him the medical records, which also included two recent mandatory treatments.

The same treating psychiatrist received phone calls from a policeman and the family doctor, both of this tone: "Forget about Mr. A. Do not torture him with your practices. He actually gets along well with others and looks great."

Here is the letter sent by A:

> *Stories of mandatory treatments, or how to reduce a human being to a shred. In the Country of ASLOV in INCUSCENTIA, one thing is certain: psychiatry has not made any progress. It remains, in fact, anchored in the medieval medicine. The bonds of restraint of that era have been replaced by lethal drugs that make apathetic those who are obliged to take them against their will.*
>
> *The mandatory treatment is kind of a life sentence, for he who suffers it remains with the indelible mark that announces to the whole world his alleged mental instability; in short, it tells everyone that he/she is an almost "crazy" individual, then different, then dangerous.*

These beings have sometimes stumbled into the rigors of this so unfair law, blameless, and above all, without being sick. They simply had some very normal inconvenient rage that made them dangerous to the interests of some people who, to avoid even economic losses, called the police complaining that they suffered serious threats. These representatives of the law address "the doctor of the insane" who, having heard the narration of the facts, without saying many words, sticks a needle into the backside of the poor fellow and injects a deadly dose of drugs. From that moment, that individual becomes a kind of zombie, always blackmailable ("...If you do not do what I tell you, I send you back to the crazy hospital"), deprived of his dignity, of his own will, of his pride of being.

Yet, at least sometimes, it would have sufficed talking, or one or more sessions led by a serious psychologist and able to understand...Are we kidding? You know how much it would cost! Better a massive dose of drugs!

Here, this is a story of poor people and illustrious graduates who shall decide the fate of others without hesitation whatsoever. Society accepts, tolerates, pretends not to see, not to hear, and so does not speak. In short, this Society plays "the three Monkeys."

All this takes us back to mind countries like those of ROSSIA, KILE, or even old TEUTONIA, where dissidents were, by law, defined crazy and, as such, were dulled chemically and sent to work as volunteers, in the roughest places of those EMPIRES. And while the dispensers of the chemicals were filled with honors and sinecures, the Users of that treatment, reduced to the rank of unsuspecting helots, were also affected by the ostracism of the rest of Society. It is useful to remember that in some cases the chemical may be temporarily useful; but what is the discriminating? And to the poor souls who have suffered as innocent the treatment, whoever brings back the lost dignity and respect for others? MEDITATE, PEOPLE, MEDITATE!

Tomorrow it could even happen to you, too, with great joy
of the ass-piercers. It's a nice story, True? Let's try not to relive
it forever.

2. Case "B"

Case "B" is a fifty-year-old doctor in charge of a mental-health service
who was trained in a collateral psychodynamic school. He had already
been fired from the health authority of another region because of his
questionable ways, his absences, and his imperviousness to any corpo-
rate directive and criticism. He was then hired back with the payment of
damages, given his tenacious defense of his own actions. He was hired by
another health authority for his political merits—very good at making
long and seemingly complicated speeches with detailed pseudoknowl-
edge of health matters and beyond.

He was able to immediately exercise forms of control over his staff
by shadowing them to verify the actual work they did. Everything was
approved in meetings, in which he decided, in practice, on everything,
leaving the others only the possibility of approving his strategies. He
took "revenge" in terms of bureaucratic controls on the dissenters, who
soon disappeared one way or another. A pseudodialectic actually left
little room for any contribution to the understanding of the circumstances: he was the only one who knew what to do and centered everything on himself.

In reality, the center was inefficient, the patients were left on their
own, and checks on staff only exacerbated their low spirits and discour-
aged them from taking initiatives. Fear reigned.

He even managed to prevent the others from using a rehabilitation
facility under his responsibility that had only one patient. This lonely
patient was actually supported by a huge staff: nurses, educators, and
psychologists. He sent a lot of letters to the management. With threatening but evanescent citations of laws and regulations, he proposed
incredibly strict inclusion criteria so that in practice almost no patient
could be admitted into his facility. Furthermore, when the ward where

patients from the community were admitted was renovated, he received approval to hospitalize them in another service, where his colleagues showed a great sense of responsibility and solidarity, since they were not obliged to do so. He strenuously refused, though, to reciprocate the solidarity, with ridiculous pseudoarguments (see letter below). He did not even symbolically send, as he had been modestly requested, a doctor to cover only one weekly shift in the new ward. He claimed that this request was rejected by his doctors (whom he controlled and directed minutely). Note that the doctors of his service—who were not few—were now completely free for the number of hours they had previously covered. What did they do in the free time they so acquired? Only he could direct them and manage them—certainly not in a manner useful to the community but to increase his own power and personal cult.

Letter sent by B:

Dear Colleagues,

I was extremely surprised by your request that one of our doctors has to go on duty once a week at your hospital ward. This request was decisively rejected at the meeting of the operators of our group unanimously.

Under the current regulations, in fact, our mental health service is not able to deprive itself of the resources deemed essential to the "basic levels of care" in the Community of competence, which has complexity both in terms of the extent and the geographical features, as can be seen from the peculiarities attributed by the Regional Health Plan. The staff assigned to us, in fact, despite repeated requests for adjustment, is well below the due levels of care, dutifully usable by the actual and potential population, who must address them for therapeutic-care and even rehabilitation. This according to local and national parameters, as prescribed by law, and to supranational parameters, as the

WHO itself well expressed regarding psychiatry, in the definition of the tasks and the user-staff relationship. And you must have in mind that all this is just in relation to the definition of minimal levels and certainly not optimal institutional care.

I wonder whether the colleagues who have made this request have seriously thought about the possible devastating consequences that could arise from a further lowering of the threshold for welfare tasks institutionally assigned to our service by the state institutions and the covenant of ethics to which each of us professionals is morally obliged. We have to follow the Hippocratic tradition and modern issues of health policy derived from the innovation of Basaglia, centered on respect for the psychologically disturbed person as a citizen whose rights and contractuality is not dissimilar from that of all subjects humanly endowed with "natural" rights and legal and social capability. This obviously implies a respect for the person to be highlighted especially in not discriminating and labeling him, also in terms of a decreased attention to his/her demands of care and performance rate that could lead to a path of rehabilitation and resocialization. This is required for his/her full participation in social life, not in the sense of a lack of proper consideration of his/her specific condition, but of attention to quality of life, in the direction indicated by the WHO itself, which defines health not as the absence of disease, but as a right to the welfare and enjoyment of all that can allow it, without limitation.

3. Case C

"C" was a forty-five-year-old criminal lawyer who was successful and well-known in his field. He was hospitalized for depression in his youth and was considered "strange" by family members. He had a "stormy" personality, with a tumultuous affective life that included divorce and turbulent relationships.

Even at work, where he showed undoubted intelligence and professional capacity, he began to experience strange connections between criminal offenses under his professional duties and in the national news. The plot included intelligence services, CIA, and so forth. The likelihood of what he claimed with strong vehemence and tenacity seemed inconsistent from the outside. He also talked about recordings and sexual violence that took place against his partner just as she left the apartment and that he "witnessed," according to him, by recordings. In the recordings, nothing is picked up except modest background noise related to audio disturbance.

He began to contact prosecutors, authorities, and councils of lawyers, including colleagues in the plot. Finally, an expert was called upon to check his mental state. He was believed to suffer from multiple personality disorder. (Alas! What the *DSM* allows and probably the fear of psychiatrists to look too directly at him—a man who analyzed in minute detail what was written about him.) He also underwent a mandatory medical treatment, which he fiercely challenged. Not at all pleased with his own expert who allegedly participated in the conspiracy against him, he then addressed a specialist suggested to him by "friends." He railed against the specialist, too, when, upon submitting the report written for his defense to the minutest criticism, he detected misconduct and attempts to discredit him, such as the elevation of the score of some scales in the psychodiagnostic tests such as hysteria and obsessions-compulsions, as are frequently found using that specific test (*Millon's Clinical Multiaxial Inventory III*) for legal assessments. He forced his lawyer to intervene, and, through a series of phone calls, he demanded the removal of the collected material, threatening retaliation. He wanted a report that was effectively conceived by him and that enhanced his personality and denied any element of psychiatric disorder.

Meanwhile, he became an "opinion leader," preparing sites and organizations for the rights of citizens on the Internet, in which he mobilized an army of followers who commented on the truth he proclaimed and railed against those who tried to limit him. He was invited to conferences and conventions almost everywhere in the country, where he attacked psychiatrists, his bitter enemies, in particular and extended the boundaries of the increasingly global conspiracy against the whole of society. His lectures, carried out vehemently, were very long. He did not respect the time limits, thinking he might expand his speech at will, and he was boring. The arguments, even in the many documents he produced, were actually poorly built, lacked common logic, and were shared with difficulty. The "job" in which he had excelled now seemed tarnished, leaving only room for pseudolegal arguments.

4. Case D

Case "D" is a forty-seven-year-old woman with two sisters and a brother. She led a normal life until high school, although it was characterized by a poor social life. She had experiences of low self-esteem, exclusion, and fear of others. She had a previous history of depression, without seeking the treatment of specialists, and psychogenic disorders (anorexia and bulimia). In her fantasies, she tended to divide the world between the persecuted and the persecutors. She was a holder of firearms and a frequenter of the shooting range.

In late 2003, she committed the nonsensical heinous murder by multiple stab wounds of a woman she had never met. The woman was the wife of a pharmacist, a former university classmate of D's whom she had lost touch with for years and found through the Internet.

The "super-expert" appointed by the judge concluded:

> *Certainly D is a mentally disturbed woman, but…her complex personality disorder is documented by medical history and the findings of our psychodiagnostic investigation. In light of what preceded, accompanied, and followed her crime, the latter did not occur in a qualitatively or quantitatively sufficient way to confer value of a disease to the crime she committed.*

This ridiculous underestimation of psychopathology in the paranoiac brings us back to the great insights of Dostoyevsky (*The Brothers Karamazov*, 1880) on the contribution of doctors (and perhaps psychologists) in the assessment of the judge. "The intervention of doctors were rather ridiculous because of the differences of opinion among them. We no longer find the doctors of a time who took care of all diseases. Now there are only specialists who sponsor themselves at full blast in the newspapers." In modern times, we would also say on TV.

"What is the alteration?" Dostoyevsky asks ironically. "Alteration, in the legal sense, for which you forgive everything. Whatever you have done."

Previous conduct of D:

- Report by a doctor (nine years before the murder) who had practiced minor surgery on her of damage to his front door
- Report by her boss at work (five years before the murder) of missing office files, harassing phone calls, and a fire at his house
- Complaints by two workmates (a man and a woman) for numerous harassing, offensive phone calls

Subjective experiences of D:

> I've attacked him [the surgeon] although he had made nothing wrong. I was angry with all, but the doctor was the only one with whom I had had contact...After that report, they took away my firearms, then I bought a knife that I always carried with me, because it gave me a sense of security and made me feel stronger...I sank into a deep depression crisis...I saw all black, I saw myself on the losing side...I saw the others, though, winning and happy. I felt it like an unjust thing...At the university I met [the pharmacist]. I remember he was a nice guy, he was the only one to treat me well, maybe even had a liking for me. Once he asked me if we studied together...Then I saw him...I knew he was a pharmacist...because the year before, I had a contest and I went on the website of the university...surfing

through the site, I saw that you could see the thesis of gradu-ates...of my classmates...via the Internet...I saw where he was working...So one day, I went to the street where there was his office, and I saw him. When I saw him, I was taken by a sort of fixation. I was reminded of the past. I began to fantasize that he had a happy life, he belonged to the class of the lucky ones and Winners...

I focused on my littleness, I felt increasingly defeated...the mood of bitterness...The negative fantasies focused on him and his wife...and...she is on the winning side...they had had that joyful life from which I was excluded...Anger, aggressiveness, envy accumulated...That morning...I had inside of me my ag-gressive fantasies, I had a whole attitude that I needed to shel-ter from bad feelings...I did not know what I would do...when she opened the door I just...it exploded all over...Then I just re-member the blood, the pain at the hands because of the wounds.

Dostoyevsky goes on:

It may happen that the alteration strikes a man not at all crazy, all of a sudden. He may be conscious and know what he is do-ing, and yet be in a state of alteration.

They discovered the alteration when they set up the new courts. It's all a positive effect of the new court.

He killed without realizing it: indeed...realizing everything, but without knowing what he was doing. To be acquitted! It would be so human an act, apt to show what a beautiful in-stitution the new courts are. He might be employed as a "judge of peace"...because those who have suffered a misfortune know better how to judge.

And then, who does not suffer from alterations in these days: you, me, we're all at the mercy of the alteration.

D had been subjected to treatment, and the results were not contemptible, but she abandoned them herself.

- D stated, "I took drugs...then I was better, and I did not go any more to the doctor."
- D also stated, "After being better and being cured...in October, this mood of anger and depression has come back."
- The treating psychiatrist said, "From the first meeting...she was a paranoiac...Gloomy, aggressive, introverted. I prescribed antipsychotics that produced, in the two subsequent meetings, some improvement."

CHAPTER 7

LEGAL PROBLEMS: EVALUATION OF EMPATHY

We make judiciary, functional, and lay judgments. They don't have to be ethical or metaphysical or about value. The judgment has an operational nature—that is, it consists of the description of the application and the results of an interdisciplinary process (organic and psychodiagnostic) and not in the expression of a moral judgment on the person. The idea of free will, of freedom of self-determination, is put in brackets.

Empathy should be seen not as a moral virtue or as something that the person is required to hold and use but as a behavioral trait to be evaluated in combination with evidence of organic and psychometric character, both for the purposes of an adjustment (pedagogical, targeted intervention) and for the purposes of assessment of dangerousness.

Hierarchies and conflict of legal interests exist. The constitutions of several countries recognize many legal goods—values that the state must protect: life, health, liberty, security, dignity, and so forth.

Often conflicts of legal interests occur, such as the protection of health and freedom. For example, the former prevails until the conditions exist for mandatory treatment. Between property protection and national economy protection, the former prevails until the conditions for expropriation are produced.

In our case, a conflict exists between the legal right of an individual's privacy and unrestrained evaluations and treatments on one side—and, on the other side, the legal interests threatened by possible and future antisocial behavior.

The citizen is free to be and remain devoid of empathy and cannot be discriminated against (deprived of opportunities or forced into treatment) simply by not having it. We don't have an ethical or psychological model of man that is canonized in the constitution. The latter does not prescribe how man should be.

CHAPTER 8

SHARED PARANOIA

S hared paranoia includes limited forms (known as *folie à deux*, or shared madness, in which symptoms of a delusional belief are transmitted from one individual to another) and forms of social involvement (multiple madness, such as the paranoia of religious sects and mass paranoia—"crazy" dictators who involve entire populations in their delusions). A summary from *Neuroschiavi* (*Neuro-Slaves*), written with Marco Della Luna, suitably treats the argument:

> *Enlarged paranoia extends to forms of persuasion, plagiarism, brainwashing, manipulation of minds made up by sects, etc. (diagnosable as a form of induced paranoia, of multiple madness). In these cases, we have to consider: 1) an inducer of psychosis (the paranoiac, the fanatic, the leader of the sect) and 2) the subject receptive in accepting the delusional system as his own, characterized mostly by weak personality and suggestibility.*

The consequences of this are not simple matters of conversations among armchair experts and, instead, relate closely to us all. The practical question is: are the paranoiacs crazy, sometimes dangerous people we must try to cure or are they normal people, though harassing, irritable, and bad, who are capable of discernment and must be resisted, if necessary, through the police and the judicial system?

We have to focus on the health aspects, in particular, concerning the management of the public and forensic services. The best treatment must necessarily take into account the many difficulties that these individuals pose. Indeed, they feel healthy, misunderstood, and persecuted. They are sent for treatment by third parties (social workers, police, or judicial authorities) as they are not aware of their disorder. They do not easily accept treatment and tend to manipulate professionals and strangers. They are particularly convincing about their reasons thanks to their hypertrophic dialectical ability, based on the use of loopholes and specious, evocative arguments.

In the face of religious beliefs, which position do we take? Religious beliefs, dogmas, and the experiences connected to them have alleged reality as their object or assumption: gods, demons, paradise, hell, souls, saints, angels, metempsychosis (the supposed transmigration at death of the soul of a human being or animal into a new body of the same or a different species), and so on. They are believed to exist externally and independently compared to the thought of the believer—not sensible, not perceived, not evident, not verified realities but that are, nevertheless, believed. In fact, they can be believed with such force, even against the evidence of their inaccuracies or indemonstrability, as to sometimes condition followers to extremes—to push them to sacrifice and kill. Therefore, convictions and religious arguments, by their very nature, correspond to the concept of psychopathological paranoid delusion.

Religions do not, however, allow their believers to be diagnosed as paranoiacs, as these have thoughts and behaviors that are logical, consistent, and appropriate to their environments. Paradoxically, participation in delusional systems of belief can, objectively, be a tool or condition of social integration, since such systems are strongly shared by the group the subjects belong to. Consequently, participation can also be a means to ensure the intrapsychic cohesion of the subject.

Yet we could think about the inclusion of disturbed individuals in a community or in a discipleship or believer-sectarianism—in a sect—as a means of therapy. Although not conclusive, in a transitional direction of harm reduction, we could get a compensation of the impaired subject, a reduction in symptoms, and a gradual entry in social and work activities.

Paranoia, as a thought disorder and a distortion of reality judgment, becomes difficult to recognize and diagnose. We distinguish it from cultural or character variables that fall within the range of normal through several factors. Among those we have mentioned are:

- The integration of the subject in a group that shares an objectively delusional faith (unreasonable and in conflict with reality), but who, outside the scope of this faith, thinks, feels, and acts in a fair and consistent way.
- The specialized nature of the topics covered by reasoning under observation: psychiatrists or psychologists are often in trouble when dealing with suspicions of delusion within cultural areas that are unfamiliar to them, such as physics or paleontology, especially when the subjects under observation carry their arguments on with good linguistic coherence and logical sequence.
- In general, the fact that contemporary, postmodern people "know" many aspects (social, economic, scientific, political) of his or her complex and contradictory world but not through simple, direct "objective" perceptions. They confront these aspects, instead, through much less objective and unambiguous models and cultural practices, often relative and very different among them (even without considering the theory of incommensurability of scientific theories established by Paul Feyerabend).

In the presence of such situations, it is difficult or impossible to accept an intrinsic break of thinking from "reality." We must go in search of external criteria other than the internal consistency of reasoning or examination of reality. For example, we could check the rigidity of thought and affection and the capacity to understand and process criticism and irony, to assume critical attitudes and self-mocking, and to receive and process the new and unexpected.

Case of "folie à deux" (shared madness between two individuals)

A couple consisting of a sixty-year-old woman (the inducer) and her husband of almost the same age (the induced) lived in an area where a large residential complex had been built. The woman's convictions were unshakable and pointed at a large number of neighbors—those closest to her—who, she said, did not respect her property and took advantage of her hookups and pipes. She often came to such a state of arousal as to get on the balcony and insult those who came within range one by one, exposing all their supposed misdeeds against her. A lawsuit brought against her neighbors was dismissed because it was based on flimsy grounds. Repeated checks by the municipal police, which she solicited through the convinced participation of her husband, led only to a fine against the couple themselves because, in reality, they were the only ones who had committed building irregularities. On the occasion of one of these inspections, she addressed the female architect of the municipality, whom she had never seen before, accusing her of being her husband's lover.

Checks required at the public service office led to poor results. The woman and her husband supported their arguments with great vehemence and avoided checks, considering them slanderous and part of the plot against them. The woman's hospitalization, under mandatory medical treatment, produced only short-term results. When she was released, everything began as before.

The neighbors were exasperated. One sold the property just to get away from the ongoing torment. The couple's daughter, her husband, and her little girl went to live elsewhere to avoid getting involved.

After several years of impasse, the woman's husband died of heart problems, certainly in relation to the state of constant tension produced by the conflict that extended and intensified.

The Manson case

Paranoid charismatic leaders, because of their haunting narcissistic prerogatives, can totally replace any ethical basis (the superego, if you want, or the moral conscience) and any test of reality. They might also be able to push their followers to commit acts that are not only ridiculous but also supremely reprehensible against the ethics of common society. Paradigmatic is the case of Charles Manson, whose devotees coolly and calmly, without manifesting any internal conflicts, told how in 1969 they had slaughtered Sharon Tate and the baby she was expecting along with other unfortunates. Manson led his followers to believe in the most absurd, ridiculous, and outlandish doctrines, behaving as though they were factually correct and denying rational capacity (*credo quia absurdum est*, meaning "I believe because it is absurd").

Those who enter into such communities are primarily, it is well-known, immature people in about their twenties who have difficulty adapting to reality with its uncertainties, insecurities, ugliness, injustice, and loneliness.

The charismatic leader offers a remedy to all this but usually aggravates the contrast with the surrounding reality so that neophytes increase their break with the world and their dependence on the group and the leader. Consequently, the group, as a whole, tends to substantially increase its contrast to the outside world, its internal cohesion, and its paranoid drift.

In parallel, the aggregated personalities tend to better adapt to each other and to the group by filing or removing individual differences in tastes, opinions, and aspirations. They also increase their unifying factors including external ones (clothing, language, idioms, and slang). The adjustment ranges from lower levels to higher ones and, at last, to the leader (those lower in the hierarchy tend to take on the traits of those above).

4. Paranoia and the Internet

A needed update on the subject of paranoia consists of the Internet, which can profoundly shape how paranoid thinking is channeled and influences developments toward society. The power of the medium is under the eyes of all, and the ability to penetrate is impressive. It is a powerful way of inducting shared paranoia.

A large number of sites of various interests (UFO and related, ecologist, nutritionist, alternative medical, pseudopolitical, pseudoscientific of various orientations, etc.) are impregnated with paranoid thought. Absolute, irrefutable truths are proclaimed on various topics and pursued with great conviction by charismatic subjects who actually attract many followers, more than humanity ever would have known until the recent past.

Around the world, people claim to telepathically channel messages of various content, mostly prophetic commanders of galactic fleets, superhuman entities, and so forth. They relaunch the channels through their websites and regular newsletters that go to the tens of thousands of followers around the world on their mailing lists. There are even sites responsible for the translation and relaunch of the bulletins in various languages. Many virtual and nonvirtual aggregations form quickly because of the booster effect of the web. They constitute cults in the sociological sense, each with its own shared experiences of truth, enlightenment, and soteriological practices.

This could become an interesting field of inquiry for psychology, sociology, and psychiatry in view of the ability of these cults to meet deep human needs. It is well-known that for many people religions no longer offer reliable answers about the meaning of life, the predictability of the future, the means to save themselves, and categorical and not relativistic criteria of ethical judgment.

These websites contain, as claimed by Marco Della Luna, "nuclei of truth, nuclei of probability, and nuclei of absurdity." This mixture of ingredients could lead to identifying the profiles of various sites of paranoid content, depending on the rating detected for each of the categories in question. That's what I propose, in a simplified manner, in the following table, which indicates a high intensity of paranoid features.

Obviously this is just a proposal, from which, however, some experimental protocol could arise. It could allow the quantitative description of a phenomenon that so far has been described only anecdotally.

Categories	Rate
Nuclei of truth	10%
Nuclei of probability	30%
Nuclei of absurdity	60%

The adepts of the sites (the induced) have many opportunities to compete with each other, to give positive reinforcement, to set up the various initiatives—often against mainstream science and those who are considered its corrupt practitioners.

There is, therefore, a third level or dimension in addition to thought and acting out: virtual acting.

Are these websites helpful or harmful? They can be both: useful, as channeling energies that remain harmlessly engaged within the theories of the site; harmful when and if the spark that can ignite goes beyond the environment where it was formed and infects the external environment (see also aggressive and violent environmental actions). They are like electrical capacitors that hold the charge up to a certain point, after which sparks, which can have an explosive effect, are formed.

In my personal experience, I have found at least one case of paranoid disorder that is far more serious than those described by Doidge (loss of attraction to the usual partner and sexual impotence), whose onset is probably linked to the discovery of porn websites. A good middle-aged official who was married with no previous homosexual interest suddenly developed persecutory delusional beliefs. He inferred by the gestures and facial expressions of the people around him that they were sending messages such as, "Why don't you react to the fact everyone says that you're a homosexual?" An exhausting torment resulted, extending and incrementing the feeling of siege. He was sure there was a conspiracy, with the subjective experience of an unjust discredit to his person, and, for the first time in his life, he sought a specialist for help. After the initial approach, in which nothing came out, he revealed that he had been visiting porn sites. Presumably, along the lines of Doidge (2007), in the vastness of the proposals offered by the various videos, his curiosity was aroused. It was lying in a remote corner of his psyche until that moment and concerned homosexual practices, which troubled him. Reinforcement due to the repetition and the craving produced by addiction brought the whole to a much more intense level, enough to disrupt the stability of his psychic system.

Still quoting Doidge:

> *Does the Net simply reveal quirks and kinks, or does it also help create them? I think it creates new fantasies out of aspects of sexuality that have been outside the surfer's conscious aware-ness, bringing these elements together to form new networks... such fantasies take hold of the mind because of the individual components in them...Hardcore porn unmasks some of the early neural networks that formed in the critical periods of sexual de-velopment and brings all these early, forgotten, or repressed ele-ments together to form a new network, in which all the features are wired together.*

All this may well extend to other types of fantasies, which would have remained hidden and harmless in the psychic background if someone had not activated them by visiting these particular websites.

CHAPTER 9

MODERN VIEWS

As previously stated, the essential feature in paranoia is not the presence of delusion but the alteration of reasoning that certainly, in the most significant cases, may reach delusion.

The classical conception of paranoia departed from the latter, being the delusion of persecution considered a form of lucid, systematized delusion—that is, manifesting in the normal state of consciousness, with characteristics of organization and articulation.

What's the "alteration of reasoning," as emphasized by Lacan, at the base of paranoia? I propose to follow three modern theories.

1. The theory of the neuropsychologist Chris Frith

According to Frith (1992, 2007), who conducted specific research on the subject, what ultimately leads to the formation of a delusion can be found in:

- Impairment of logical processes of deduction and inference (poorly confirmed by empirical data);
- Perceptual abnormalities—that is, when the subject applies normal logic to a distorted experience or perception (but this situation does not apply well in the case of paranoia); and
- Abnormal use of information derived from normal perceptions and experiences.

This would be the case in question. "Basically, this means that some information is ignored, while others are emphasized excessively."

Brennan and Hemsley (1984) maintain that the abnormal paranoid thinking follows the same mechanisms that underlie the associations in normal people, which are frequently biased. People often believe in nonexistent relationships between events because they do not give enough value to counterexamples. In other words, once they draw the hypothesis (in response to random coincidences), they maintain it despite evidence to the opposite. Frith quotes Sterne (1760), according to whom:

> *The nature of the hypothesis, once it is conceived by man, is to assimilate all to it, as its own food; and from the first moment it is generated, usually grows and becomes stronger through all that is seen, heard, read, or understood. This phenomenon is very frequent.*

In part, it may, therefore, be an exaggerated form of this natural tendency. The aforementioned Brennan and Hemsley (1984) found that paranoid patients perceived illusory associations between pairs of words that randomly appeared together, in particular when these words were associated with their delusions. Hemsley and Garety (1986) suggested that some delusions result from deficits in the ability to evaluate new evidence and take in the resulting convictions. Paranoiacs, therefore, have an impaired ability to produce assessments based on probability. This was also confirmed by other studies, in the sense that patients with these characteristics were overly confident about the conclusions drawn from limited information.

The interesting thing is that the alterations of thought present in these individuals seem to relate only to their placement in the social universe. Consequently, their incorrect reasoning compromises only their understanding of human interactions, their social reasoning.

At this point, it should be reiterated that the human brain is a tool designed for adaptation to the environment, and it works very differently from a computer, as far as we now know. Accuracy of calculation is not one of its main objectives. Instead, knowing how to manage ourselves in a society of peers, being able to differentiate between when to approach (possible reward) and when to distance (risk of punishment). In other words, the proper application of logic is not a common feature of human thought. Most issues are resolved on the basis of the knowledge that comes from experience rather than by reasoning. Paranoid patients try to apply logic in circumstances where normal people would not. The impairment of the cognitive processes that are important for social reasoning would, thus, be the basis for the abnormal thinking of paranoiacs.

2. The theory of neuroscientist Kathleen Taylor

Neuroscientist Kathleen Taylor developed the system of "cogwebs" (cognitive webs). This term indicates the models that unify patterns, beliefs, and neural substrate (organic basis).

In her book *Brainwashing* (2004), she developed the metaphor of water channels to explain the functioning of the brain, as summarized in *Neuroschiavi* (*Neuro-Slaves*, 135):

> The new incentives will travel the network of existing channels, preferring the larger and more concentrated ones, and modifying mostly the closest, isolated, peripheral ones. However, if the existing channels fail to absorb the supervening flow, the system is in crisis and different solutions become possible:
>
> a) the energy flow can widen violently some channels, modify the network;
> b) or open new ones;

> *c) or the strong-convictions systems react, defending them-*
> *selves, through an adaptation of the signal, which modifies*
> *it to make it compatible with themselves; and they do this*
> *through the regulation of subcortical filters.*

So Taylor goes on:

> *The weakest cogwebs tend to modify in response to inputs*
> *that contradict them...are subjected to reality. The strongest*
> *cogwebs tend to modify the inputs which contradict them—*
> *and they can lead to the formation of new cogwebs to clear*
> *the new information. Here reality is subjected to expecta-*
> *tions. People differ in the ease with which they accept new*
> *information that contradicts existing beliefs...but overall,*
> *the tolerance threshold seems lower than we like to assume.*
> *Humankind cannot bear a large part of reality...As many*
> *psychological experiments have shown, often you see what*
> *you expect to see. We also can be amazingly ingenious in*
> *rejecting unwelcome facts.*

The principle is, therefore, that a subject's beliefs are not all the same: they are central or marginal, strong or weak, posited or derived, emotionally charged or not, conscious or unconscious. In a threatening situation (attack on the stability of the system), the central cogweb can exercise a strong resistance. In extreme cases, you can get to psychotic conditions.

In paranoia, a particular difficulty can be assumed to exist in accepting new information that could conflict with existing beliefs, modifying them (i.e., distorting them) to make them compatible with the system. The consequence is that any new input, of whatever kind it is, will only confirm the basic beliefs that form the unshakable central cogweb, which regulates everything.

3. The theory of Mark Johnson

Mark Johnson, professor of liberal arts and sciences, in his interesting book *The Meaning of the Body* (2007), offers some considerations that may well be used to expand our knowledge on the subject in question:

> *...meaning includes qualities, emotions, percepts, concepts, images, image schemas, metaphors, metonymies, and various other imaginative structures. Learning the meaning of something would thus include a growing sense of all the qualities, percepts, distinctions, recollections of what has gone before, and anticipations of possible future experience that follow from it. No isolated thing, percept, or quality has any meaning in itself. Things, qualities, events, and symbols have meaning for us because of how they connect with other aspects of our actual or possible experience. Meaning is relational and instrumental.*

And more:

> *Things and events have meaning by virtue of the way they call up something beyond them to which they are concerned. This selection or partial taking from the continuous flow of experience that lies at the heart of meaning is, on the one hand, the means of the very probability of fruitful investigation, symbolic interaction, and communication; on the other hand, it simultaneously requires us to ignore the nonselected aspects of a situation. What we emphasize and, conversely, what we ignore will make all the difference in what things mean to us. Abstraction is a great tool for the furtherance of human inquiry, but it is also responsible for much of the loss of meaning that is available to us in any given situation...In other words, continued processes of abstraction...do not always bring us closer to the fullness of a situation; they may take us farther from its full meaning. Hence,*

our individual and collective habits of grasping the meaning of anything via abstraction will fatefully determine how our world stands forth for us. And if our philosophies—our most comprehensive accounts of the meaning of things—are grounded on the most partial and superficial aspects of experience, then our entire understanding of life will be drastically impoverished. It thus makes all the difference whether we take experience in the limited sense, as meaning things as known or conceptualized, or whether we take it in its fullness, as redolent with meaning that surpasses our undoubtedly useful abstractions from it. Part of philosophy's job is to help us recover the fullest possible meaning of our experience—the pulsating, lived world that transcends any conceptual specification of it. (269–270)

In accordance with Frith, we can infer that, in paranoia, there is an exaggerated tendency to apply logic and abstraction to experience, which should instead be grasped freely, without preconceived structures, in order to be adaptive.

4. Reflections from the three theories considered, with the support of neuroscience

The goals of human existence and subjective intentions involve information and knowledge on the objectives themselves. The latter type of knowledge, as Frith recalled, is an example of "metarepresentation" (second order of representation). Without the ability of metarepresentation, behavior becomes stereotyped and persevering.

Once self-awareness is reached, the child can perform the task in reverse with much more efficiency. When the reverse occurs, the child not only is aware that the goal was not achieved, but is also aware of the intention that led him to this failure.

Consequently, he is able to remove this inappropriate action and quickly find a new correct action.

The metarepresentation is the cognitive mechanism that allows us to be aware of our goals, our intentions, and the intentions of others.

In paranoia, there is a defective awareness of the intentions of others. There is an inability to correctly *read* the mental states of others so that their intentions are interpreted in a distorted way, such as arguing that there is a conspiracy against them, a will to deceive.

In addition, they understand well the value of deception, they will try to deceive and think that others are deceiving them. Because they do not infer correctly the convictions of the person they are cheating, their attempts will be easily discovered. On the other hand, they won't be persuaded that they are wrong, in the belief that others are deceiving them. (Frith, 129–130)

The deficit in the ability to read the mental states of others can be reported at the neurological level, to the brain system for social cognition, mapped in the metarepresentation: the temporal cortex and the amygdala provide crucial information for the content of the propositions, while the overall metarepresentation requires that these structures interact with the frontal cortex.

For intentional actions as well as for social cognition, the appropriate metarepresentation may depend on an interaction between the prefrontal cortex and those parts of the brain that deal with the primary representation, namely with the content of the proposition ("I mean, I think, I know").

CHAPTER 10

CRITERIA TO EVALUATE A PARANOIAC

As stated previously, the paranoiac is not so difficult to detect by a common citizen but is often a serious problem for a psychiatrist who has to provide diagnostic "evidence."

At present, possible developments of great interest are substantially still limited at the research phase in the specific sector: neuroimaging techniques such as CT scan and brain MRI that highlight anatomical anomalies; PET and SPECT, which examine brain function in metabolical terms; intracranial stimulation techniques such as TMS, which can provide neurophysiological elements; and the kit for the detection of genetic profiles. The method still used in psychiatry remains the clinical interview, possibly supported by the administration of psychodiagnostic tests.

In the case of paranoiacs, we are faced with people who don't consider themselves sick. On the contrary, they believe they are persecuted so that the clinical examination itself is included in this context. Interviews are difficult, marked by their deep distrust. They will certainly not try to respond with spontaneity. The psychiatrist will be faced with emotionally controlled subjects (except for a few moments of impatience with having to undergo the interview). The subjects are rigid in their beliefs, show no empathy in the sense that their impenetrable worlds remain emotionally closed, and communicate little. They do not seem interested in the condition of their neighbors.

It is useless to investigate the delusion: paranoiacs strongly support their motives with that shabby logic that we considered before and will not admit to being contradicted, even with rational arguments, common sense, and courtesy. The ones who oppose them automatically become their enemies.

The scheme prepared by Lavoine (1998) (see below) gives much guidance on the course on which the psychiatrist should conduct a much more thorough exploration than usual, collecting information from family, acquaintances, and so forth. As in the clinical case D, we often find many previous episodes of disturbed behavior. It also provides guidance on what to look for in the paranoiac's behavior and the nonempathetic relationship with the expert.

The paranoiac will perform well on psychodiagnostic generic tests, as they are conceived today. Nonprojective personality tests (answers to questions) like the *MMPI-RV* and Millon's *MCM-III* will be considered valid—the scales that should affect validity are not compromised—and will result in normal values on the clinical scales for paranoia-persecution. Sometimes, but not always, other scales have high scores, such as the hysterical, obsessive-compulsive, affective (manic-depression) scales. One explanation is that the patient is attentive to what answers to choose by considering the protocol in detail, scouring it, and not responding spontaneously, usually taking much more time than usual in the compilation.

Projective personality tests such as Rorschach's, still applied in Italy, have been criticized for their validity (see *Italian Treaty of Psychiatry*). In the United States, the Rorschach Comprehensive System has been considered by W. M. Grove and R. C. Barden (1999) as inadmissible for expert psychological testimony according to the guidelines from the Daubert (1993), Joiner (1997), and Kumho (1999) decisions.

Specific scales for paranoia were drawn, such as the Paranoia Scale by Fenigstein and Vanable and the Self-Consciousness Rating Scale by Scheier and Carver, but these are not useful in highlighting specific psychopathological elements.

The element we must, instead, concentrate on is empathy, along with texts written by the paranoiac. We can detect empathy from our own experiences during the interviews, as well as through some questionnaires. In particular, I consider IRI (Interpersonal Reactivity Index) by Mark H. Davis (1983, 1994).

An even more interesting way to assess empathy is by applying objective tests on the variation of the emotional state following standard audiovisual stimulation (IAPS) and recording psychophysiological variables using appropriate equipment. In practice, we show on a screen, one after the other, a series of emotion-provoking images (acoustic stimuli can also be used) and objectively record the psychophysiological responses of the subject.

With psychophysiological tests, we assess and quantify the responses evoked by somatic and visceral stimuli with affective valence (positive, neutral, negative) of increasing intensity, presented according to the visual and/or acoustic mode. The responses studied are the sympathetic autonomic system (sympathetic skin response), changes in heart rate and plethysmography, alteration of pupil size, and electromyographic activity. Event-Related Potentials (ERPs) can also be recorded from the scalp in response to stimuli of emotional valence. The responses are measured, subject to standardization procedures and statistical evaluation, and are compared with those obtained in a population of normal subjects. The psychophysiological measures so recorded are then inserted into a grid of individual patient evaluation. This psychophysiological protocol can easily be conducted in the laboratory with a relatively small commitment of time (two hours for the registration of all the above parameters).

Different levels of emotional dysfunction are characteristic of all psychopathological conditions, and, in particular, the empathetic ability may well be put in evidence.

The detection of the highlights of the course (historical data collected by third parties) and the approach to the interview (following, for example, Lavoine's scheme, below), the examination of written products (and the logic applied to issues of interest), along with the survey by questionnaire and psychophysiological tests of empathy can lead to the determination of a psychopathological profile that, with good approximation, can give us an indication of an index of paranoia expressed as a percentage of probability.

Lavoine's Scheme (1998): psychoses developing with "low noise" (how to detect a psychotic disorder since its prodromal phase).

- In the behavior some signs of inappropriateness are detectable.
- Emotional detachment in social relationships
- Passivity toward life events (without integration into them)
- Periods of isolation and depression
- Thought disorder (ruminations, bizarre rationalizations)
- Behavioral mismatch: alcoholization, deviant and impulsive behavior (sex, wandering), clastic crises (wrathful and maladjusted reactions, absurd aggressions), seclusion, attempted suicides
- Important contrast between the severity of behavioral disorders and mode of speech (cold, neutral, banalizing) with inability to logically justify the conduct and to allow himself to be emotionally involved

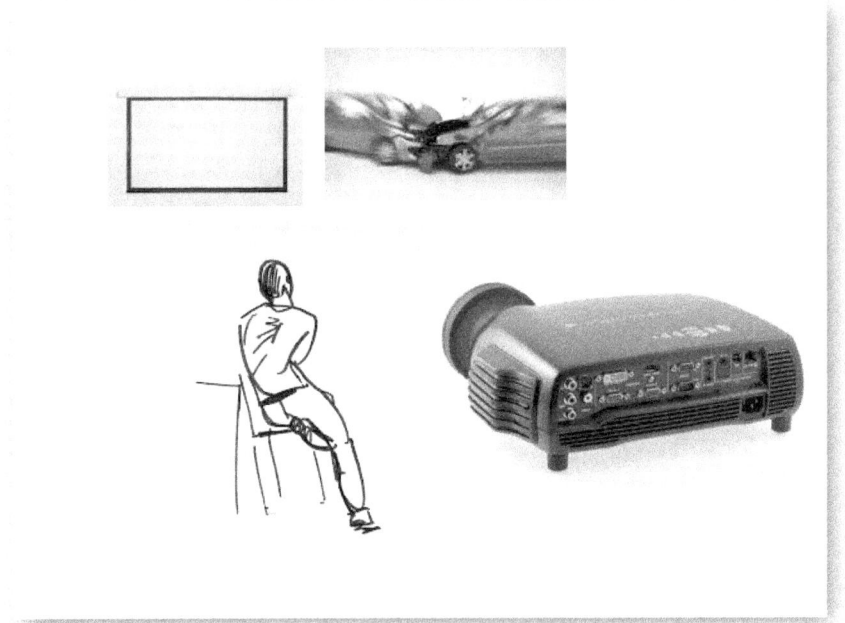

CHAPTER 11

THE TREATMENT

Paranoiacs can be considered more difficult to treat, because:

- They are sent only at the request of third parties (social services, family doctors, neighborhood, police, etc.) when their behavior becomes particularly disturbing and is the subject of social alarm;
- They do not easily accept treatment and tend to manipulate professionals and strangers;
- They consider themselves as healthy, misunderstood, and persecuted and have little or no awareness of the disease;
- They are particularly convincing about their own reasons, which they tend to strongly defend with undoubted skills;
- They have a hypertrophic dialectical skill (although it is certainly not based on an iron logic and is supported, instead, with great fervor and unlimited tenacity) based on the use of loopholes and specious arguments.

In the acute condition, it is appropriate for the person concerned to seek the psychiatrist's intervention in order to:

- Consider the opportunity of mandatory medical treatment at hospitals when the psychiatrist deems the situation urgent (such as the possibility of striking actions, hetero- or self-directed);

– Remove the patients from their environments as a therapeutic, inevitable, and effective priority.

The forms of psychiatric treatments are based on the most present characteristics of the profile:

– Lack of reasoning: antipsychotics. Intramuscular, long-acting medications, when compliance with therapy is particularly poor and the access to the patient is difficult. In practice, it is found that, at least in some cases, psychotropic drugs have more effect than one might pessimistically predict (see, for example, clinical case D).
– Expansion of the ego (affective disorders predominate): mood stabilizers, antidepressants, and anxiolytics (see Cioni, Poli, 2007)
– Loneliness and unsociability: rehabilitation support and community intervention
– A wide range of actions, ranging from damping raised social and relational issues with possible mediation with the neighborhood and public authorities. I remember that once I had to organize a "condo meeting" at the mental-health service facility in order to "defend" my patient.
– Continuous monitoring of the clinical condition and control of the administration of treatment (nurses at home, etc.)
– Use of intermediate facilities (group homes, etc.) to support a possible diurnal or residential support

Treatment outcomes

Much experience has been gained during recent years of community psychiatry activity. We are now led to believe that an integrated intervention in this type of disorder can produce much better results than the hopelessly grim prognosis formulated by the fathers of psychiatry (see also the reported case of Ernst Wagner). The psychopharmaco-logical treatment of paranoia has been underestimated in the past, but the combination of an antipsychotic with a new generation antidepressant (e.g., SSRI) can also prove very effective. Of course, we must always confront the difficulties of poor compliance to therapy that is often present in these patients. In particular, drugs can be used to desensitize patients from the emotional consequences of abnormal thinking. Paranoiacs will be much less disturbed by their convictions and will not react emotionally and impulsively, without involving sedation.

Hints for treatment

- We should aim at the practical result of neutralizing dangerous behaviors, rather than result of.
- Entering the subjects into relational networks that offer the powerful factors of reassurance and support, and targeted reinforcement that keeps them on course

The inclusion in a sect may have a paradoxical therapeutic use.

- Use the gregarious-making, aggregating effect of a religious group (or charity) that is already active.
- We could apply the "active ingredients" of a guru, for example, and transfer the dangerous ideational-impulsive nucleus material from the level of acting out to the symbolic, mythological one. From the determined dimension of here and now, to the indeterminate dimension of the cosmic game and the time of myth.
- The example of the Hare Krishna can provide guidance. They repress aggression, deny it, and then transfer it to a mythological level, in terms of gigantic battles that took place millions of years ago.

Symbolic dimension and emotional support

- A certain subset of paranoiacs are likely to commit violent acts because they have not developed the ability to transfer their aggressive mental representations into a virtual dimension. For them, the induction of experiences of symbolization and of cosmic projection could be opportunities for real recovery.
- The containment function may contribute to the stabilization of the affective component. Targeted therapy can develop this.
- To perform these inductions, we should study the propensities of the subject and exploit them. Not so much, however, the magical-religious propensities but the gregarious ones: religiosity is induced by the transference on the organized group.

What to do when you have to interact with a paranoiac

- Escape. It may seem trivial, but, when possible, it is best to withdraw from the competition and avoid getting in a tussle with a paranoiac. Points of principle have to be avoided. The result will always be negative, especially if you try to mediate and, indeed, all the more so if you try to be kind and compassionate—this can trigger the belief that the paranoiac is close to crushing the enemy, who gives a demonstration of abating. You might as well sell off the house and move, or try to change jobs. (I am aware that the objectives I suggest are difficult to attain in the present economic crisis.)
- Try using logical arguments and refer to actual laws and regulations rather than counterattacking in detail the proposed topics, which are often pseudoarguments with no legal or administrative value. However, avoid personal attacks and direct controversy.

- Avoid being identified as "the enemy" by sharing the action against the paranoiac with anyone else. This is also true for therapists: avoid offering a single interlocutor.
- Do not show fear (always being cautious, though). If you feel strong enough, you can behave "crazier" than the paranoiac without adopting the same themes. Sing vulgar songs or behave weirdly. All this may be classified as a paradoxical effect, used within the relational-systemic schools.

CHAPTER 12

CONCLUSIONS

Paranoia, the core of psychiatry, has strange relationships with the discipline. It is increasingly neglected and untreated—or even denied—by modern psychiatry, perhaps because society itself is getting more and more paranoid, and those who have the characteristics of a paranoiac become increasingly indistinguishable and tolerated. Relativism and pluralism of thoughts? Paranoid delusion as a retaliation of weak thought that does not decide on anything? It is here that the impaired thought escapes from the straitjacket of psychopathology and overpowers diagnosis to trespass and establish itself. This is done by paranoid leaders—"winners," since they are not recognized as paranoid—in the ineffable world of politics, of religion and parareligion, and of pseudoscience and social philosophies molded to size.

In times of systemic crisis and radical uncertainties, perhaps the worst threat to civilization is the charisma of delusional leaders—the indiscreet charm of paranoia.

Indeed, in situations of great uncertainty, the disoriented population tends to trust and follow those who radiate interpretive and planned certainties, especially if they offer simple and direct solutions with ethical anthropomorphic basis and detection of the guilty (scapegoats). The population believes and follows without analyzing if those strong certainties arise from cognitive, pathologically distorted processes. This is a serious danger of our time, a danger that is amplified by the power of communication and mass suggestion.

CHAPTER 13

FORMULATING A RATIONAL AND NONRANDOM NOTION OF PARANOIA-DELUSIONAL DISORDER

by Marco Della Luna

I t would be arbitrary to seek a rational and not arbitrary definition of "paranoia" without first explicitly formulating a method of defining rationally and not arbitrarily all mental illnesses, which funds the opportunity to say that there is a distinct nosographic entity to be defined "paranoia."

In common thinking, the notions of various mental illnesses have been formed on the model of the organic ones, which is characterized by symptomatic features objectively observable and (more or less) distinct from a known or knowable disease process and from a known or knowable pathogenic factor. For example, the notion of malaria consists of certain symptoms, produced by a specific pathogenic process, triggered by the bite of Anopheles mosquito.

The common thought notes that there are (cognitive, emotional, perceptual) behavioral dysfunctions and brings them by analogy to the concept of (organic) disease. Therefore, still through an analogic presumption present in that model, it tries to isolate and describe the various symptomatic species, their pathogenic mechanisms, and their causes.

However, this analogy, alleged by common sense, is arbitrary; it is adopted and applied implicitly, without even having placed the question whether or not it is justified. Especially since today, and only to a small extent, we start to be able to investigate the processes and the objective causes of mental disorders and also to be able to define objectively the different "diseases."

The application of that analogy, placed at the base for the construction of psychopathology and, consequently, of psychiatry and clinical psychology (excluding some schools), has led to unsustainable results. We are confronted with indefinability or arbitrariness or ambiguity or poor accessibility or easy confusion of the various nosographic figures. The choice of a "democratic" method (*DSM*) has not improved things.

I propose the following general method:

1) Logging events (signs and symptoms, isolated or connected) on the basis of objectively recognizable dysfunctionality (e.g., tics, incontinence, unreasonableness) or subjectively enunciated (moodiness, intrusive ideas, hallucinations, lack of emotion);

2) Checking the correlations between the various events so registered, in order to identify and describe the statistically significant groups, and specifying the degree of statistical significance of each group;

3) Checking the correlations with organic signs and symptoms, as well as with known organic processes and with other objective factors (age, sex, race, education level, significant accidents of life, use of drugs, etc.) in order to ascertain and measure the degree of significance of correlations;

4) Taking into account the parameter "dividuality"—that is, the fact that a person, physically unique, can "accommodate" multiple subpersonalities or have split or situational personalities and that, in any case, the structure of the personality is not unique and constant. Then traits and syndromes may vary with changes of the personality structure;

5) Proceeding, according to the results obtained as above, to the formulation of a general classification of mental diseases. This latter will be defined as empirical-statistical-syndromic, waiting to develop an etiological controllable understanding.

Moving on, in particular, to paranoia, I expect that by the operations described above, a syndrome or more syndromes will jump out that we feel we can apply this designation.

The core of this type of syndrome suggests that it is defined in relation to dysfunctions in adjustment (in performance or quality of life) due to dysfunctions of cognitive syntax and interpretation of objective observable reality. Consequently, it is not caused by noetic ("of, relating to, or based on the intellect") contents because these are phenomenologically infinite, linked to cultural variables, and sometimes have values that differ depending on how the subject has acquired them. In other words, it is different if the conviction that the world is floating on an ocean of milk results from being brought up in a Hindu culture or from being inferred through analogical interpretation from the observation of the cream that forms on fresh milk. It is also different if the denial of objectivity of time and space is placed in a quantum-mechanical or magical perspective.

The syndrome will have its formal variables, as follows:

a) Degree of organization-complexity
b) Degree of invasion of the subject's life, both synchronically and diachronically
c) Degree of impairment of the subject's ability to adapt to the external and internal needs (subjective: obstacle to affectivity, for example)
d) Degree of energy (sthenic feature)
e) Modes of reference, persecution
f) Types of produced mismatching
g) Any produced benefits (ascendancy on the other)

h) Contingent factors influencing events
i) Degree of accessibility to dialogue and reasoning
j) Degree of ability to recognize, describe, evaluate, and inhibit the features, and so forth

The distinction between paranoia-psychosis and paranoia-delusional disorder of personality seems to me quantitative, not qualitative.

I think also that many events covered in the scheme "paranoia" can be interpreted as follows.

The perception, interpretation, and interaction with objective reality and with the other, as with the subject's own life experiences, is often—without the subject's knowledge—interfered, distorted, inhibited, diverted, overwritten, or overridden by the action of endogenous factors of the subject. They derive from the subject's private history, active in the present (images, phantasmatic, transfer). The individuals, especially in certain situations with specific stimuli and links, process the actual objective situation in relation to their subjective situation. They live on, for example, and act out conflicts of their childhoods aimed at real present people (partners, associates, employers) with emotions, interpretations, and claims of their inner dynamics, relating to images and conflicts in their history.

Exiting the theater of their phantasmic history is difficult because it is implanted, with its sense of reality and with its emotional strength, before the development of the faculty of discernment-differentiation. Furthermore, it is the family theater, through bodily interactions, to form the self.

This kind of "paranoia," not necessarily falling into delusion, is perhaps conceivable as an unfinished process of self-identification and differentiation from the family theater and from the reality of the timeless scenes of that theater.

Brief Glossary of Psychiatric Terms

(Poli, E., and Cioni, P. See bibliography)

Delusion

The delusion has always been considered the essence of madness. According to a traditional definition, delusion is "a misconception that yields neither to reasoning nor to evidence, not belonging to the socio-cultural background of the subject." Three are therefore the peculiar characters of delusion, according to Jaspers: 1) conviction with an absolute sense of certainty; 2) inability to be influenced by reasoning or evidence; 3) evident absurdity of the content.

This definition characterizes delusion in its most important aspects, but it can be said that none of the three conditions are absolute. The first two are clearly related in that it is the abnormal feeling of certainty that makes the judgment refractory to external factors. The feeling of certainty is the feeling associated with the alleged possession of the truth. Indeed, the tenacity with which the patients are attached to their delusions is not always irreducible. There are various degrees of certainty, ability to take a position, to doubt, sometimes even to show self-irony. There are, on the contrary, persistent ideas, indomitable, fanatical, which are not considered delusional. For many of these (for example, religious beliefs, superstitions), it can be discriminatory that these are shared by a group or community (while delusion is typically a private conviction). In the case of personal fanatical ideas, the distinction is sometimes difficult and the morbidity of the idea is essentially suggested by the ways it is defended. The absurdity (or impossibility) of content is much less characteristic: the thought may prove unequivocally delusional even without absurdity of content. Typical is the case of some delusions of jealousy, which may have a morbid essence even if the content is plausible or even true (the patient is actually betrayed). The morbidity of the phenomenon is "suspected by the way in which the patients adduce evidence" (vague, implausible) as a demonstration of their convictions.

Often the arguments in defense of the delusional idea, when present, give the impression of secondary elaborations of an alien experience that can't be derived from common experience: "I know that it is so." Delusion has, in other words, the primary characteristics of an inner experience in which the common sense and judgment of reality (consciousness of reality) are impaired. Since reality is given to us in a network of meanings, the delusional experience is an alteration of the meaning of reality. The delusional idea can therefore be defined as "a morbid error of judgment, linked to an alteration of consciousness and perception of reality."

The first type of definition (based on the three criteria: abnormal subjective certainty, refractoriness, absurdity of the content) has an operating direction but is inaccurate. The second type of definition (morbid error due to altered consciousness of reality) is little operational, as it is not easy to define what is "morbid" but perhaps comes closest to the essence of the phenomenon. It should also be noted that in clinical practice, it is the whole psychopathological context that helps identify certain ideas as delusional: the presence of several ideas not linked to each other, the arguments used to defend them, the combination of other psychopathological symptoms (e.g., hallucinations), and, finally, the recurrence of some typical themes, all of high personal resonance and focused on the subject. The increased uncertainty in clinical psychopathology arises in cases, however rare, of single-issue, coherent, plausible ideational systems unaccompanied by other relevant psychopathological symptoms (paranoia, in Kraepelin's narrow sense).

A delusion should be distinguished from an overvalued idea (see below). Perhaps there is a continuum between some overvalued ideas and the corresponding delusions (e.g., between morbid jealousy and delusions of jealousy or between dysmorphophobia [belief that one's own appearance is unusually defective and is worthy of being hidden or fixed] and monosymptomatic hypochondriacal delusion [delusion of body dysfunctionality]).

Types of delusion

There is a substantial difference between "lucid delusion," in a state of waking consciousness, and "delirium," in an altered state of consciousness. The delirium is always fragmented, disjointed, and changeable. The lucid delusion can be more or less systematized (organized, articulate, or fragmented, consisting of isolated ideas).

The German psychopathological tradition has placed a clear limit between "primary delusion" and "secondary delusion," or "deliroid." The primary delusion is an underivable phenomenon on a psychopathological level and is incomprehensible. Among primary delusions, according to Jaspers, we find:

- "Delusional perception" (a real perception is interpreted according to an abnormal meaning, usually self-reported and highly relevant personally; e.g., "I see a bell, and this means that I am called to a great mission");
- "Delusional intuition" (the delusional idea suddenly bursts into consciousness); and
- "Delusional representation" (memories, such as an image, are invested with abnormal meaning).

Delusional perceptions are frequent in schizophrenic onsets. The primary delusion can be seemingly sudden without preparation field. Other times a mood with strong and ambiguous affective tone is reported (agitation, confusion, waiting, looming threat, sense of transformation of the world, self-reference) from which delusion germinates. This is interpreted as an effort to make sense of this enigmatic atmosphere (delusional mood or delusional atmosphere). At this level, a point of connection is conceivable between impairments in mood and thought disorders.

The secondary delusion is derivable from other psychopathological phenomena. The most frequent cases are:

a) An attempt to make sense of abnormal experiences (e.g., delusions of persecution from threatening voices; "delusional interpretations");

b) Elaboration of a primary delusion (e.g., conviction to be controlled, further processing: there is an international organization with special equipment to control the subject; "delusional elaborations");

c) Derived from an altered affective state (e.g., delusions of ruin and guilt in the depressed; "holothymic delusions"); and

d) Delusional development based on a characterogenic basis, triggered by significant events ("key events") (e.g., delusions of reference and persecution in "sensitive" subjects; characterogenic delusions).

The primary delusion has traditionally been considered peculiar of schizophrenia. On the other hand, it is always difficult to be sure that a delusion is really primary. From the provided definitions, it is also clear that the boundary between secondary delusion, false idea, and overvalued idea remains largely arbitrary. In current, purely descriptive terminology, delusions are reported as "mood congruent" or "mood incongruent" (e.g., in a manic state with delusions of grandeur or persecution, respectively).

Depression

A "depressive syndrome" is a constellation of signs and symptoms that are found to be characteristically associated in pathological depression. In the description of Kraepelin, who introduced the term, three are the essential features of the syndrome: depressed mood (flexion, sadness), ideational inhibition, and psychomotor inhibition (slowdown). It is usually emphasized the pairing sadness-slowdown, although this is not always found in clinical practice.

The alternating of depression with mania leads to manic-depressive illness or bipolar disorder.

Empathy

Empathy is identification with another person rather than mere projection. Someone with empathy is able to adapt to the reality, sensitivity, and needs of others. Empathy is the basis of social behavior, and a lack of empathy is the root cause of many antisocial behaviors. I found an interesting intuition about the lack of empathy in psychopaths in contrast with normal subjects in a novel (still in press) I read recently, which confirms what English philosopher Goldie (see bibliography) argues. He says that only gifted novelists are able to find the words to express emotions: "Very empathetic people and psychopathic people are two opposites—although they do have hypersensitivity in common. Most psychopaths are usually not empathetic because all sensitivity has to do with themselves. A psychopathic person is basically selfish and feigns empathy for another only if it yields a profit. Meanwhile, the benefit for an empathetic person is always without an ulterior motive. An empathetic person thinks, "When I can, I will do some charity," or, "Have I done something for others? Is that enough?" When psychopaths are asked to help, in order to appear sincere, they will ask themselves or ask directly, "For charity's sake? Why should I?" For them, it is about image, advertisement, and attention; never because it's considered right. That which isn't altruism is negative. Therefore, if sensitivity is constructive in the empathetic, it is destructive in psychopaths. (Klara Kutchera, see bibliography)

Hallucinations

Hallucinations are perceptions without object. Perception is the process through which the sensations become significant for the subject by suppressing irrelevant information and associating and integrating relevant information with the cognitive assets. Unlike "illusions," this is not a wrong interpretation of a real perception but *an entirely imaginary perception.* The patient hears, sees, feels things (localized in outer space) that do not exist in reality. Classically, it is said that the patient is not able to distinguish these false perceptions of reality. In fact, this is not always true. Hallucinations are almost always related to pathological situations.

Hallucinations may occur in disorders at different levels:

1) Diseases of the sense organs;
2) Psycho-organic syndromes; and
3) Functional psychoses.

The very definition of perception without object appears reductive: the hallucinatory experience globally involves the existence of the subject, in particular, often combined with the phenomenon of delusion (up to 90 percent of cases). The delusion can express an attempt to interpret abnormal perceptual experiences. It cannot be excluded, vice versa, that some delusional beliefs (e.g., of being watched, of being poisoned) are able to solicit misperceptions (more likely illusions than hallucinations). Hallucinations can affect all organs, including the widespread somatic sensation (kinesthesia) and sometimes several organs simultaneously (combined hallucinations).

- **Auditory hallucinations.** The patient hears more or less defined sounds. The voices typically aim at the subject; other times there may be a conversation of voices (voices dialoguing with each other). The voices, regardless of the sex of the patient, can be masculine or feminine, often refer to imaginary people, but sometimes are attributed to real people (a family member, a neighbor). They can be single or multiple. The voices, friendly or hostile, can advise, reassure, threaten, mock, control ("imperative hallucinations"), or comment on the behavior of the patient. Typical of schizophrenia is the phenomenon of "thought echo": voices repeat the patients' thoughts to establish a background in all their activities. These hallucinations are more common in functional psychoses (more often schizophrenia, less often manic-depressive illness). They are also found in organic and toxic conditions (alcoholism).

- **Visual hallucinations.** The patient sees mental images or even very complex, static, or animated scenes. They are typical of organic disorders, such as alcoholism: delirium tremens (vision of small animals).
- **Gustatory and olfactory hallucinations.** Patients feel unusual, mostly unpleasant tastes and smells. They are typical but not exclusive to organic conditions such as epilepsy. They are also observed in schizophrenia and less often in severe depression.
- **Somatic hallucinations.** They may cover the surface sensitivity: feeling being touched ("tactile hallucinations" such as in cocaine addicts) or feeling wet, hot, or cold ("thermal hallucinations"). They often involve the deep, kinesthetic or visceral sensitivity: sensation of movement of body parts, of flying, sinking (kinesthetic hallucinations), feeling possessed, raped ("sexual hallucinations"), painful sensations ("painful hallucinations"), visceral sensations more or less bizarre, deformation and transformation of the body (the body shrank, became stone), or of being possessed by animals (zoopathy). Hallucinations of the proprioceptive and visceral sensitivity often have the quality of imposed somatic events. They are frequent in schizophrenia. It is difficult, in these cases, to discern between perceptual experiences: whether it is hallucination or illusion and the delusional processing.

Mania

The psychopathology of mania largely mirrors that of depression: the affective, ideational, and motor weakening of the latter opposes the affective ideational and motor exaltation of the former. In terms of physical appearance, always impressive is the contrast in the same subject between the inhibited, senile appearance of the depressive phase and the youthful exuberance of the manic phase. Paranoia was previously called "cold mania" to indicate the presence of the only component of chronic exaltation of thought separated from other aspects of acute mania.

Obsessive Idea

There are ideas that intrude into consciousness so insistently that the persons cannot free themselves even if they are aware of their absurdity. The subjects also realize that the obsessions are the product of their own minds and are not imposed from outside. The content of these ideas is variable, even in the same subject, but there are some recurring themes: moral scruples, religious, sexual, fear of contamination, ideas of order and symmetry. Sometimes excruciating thoughts intrude, contrary to the subjects' morality (blasphemous ideas, ideas of damaging someone). Compulsions may come along, which are behaviors that reassure the subject from the intruding ideas (to defend from the anxiety produced by them: e.g., check if they tuned off the stove or the space heater). In turn they may take a repetitive, stereotyped, more or less elaborate direction (obsessive rituals). Sometimes compulsions occur apparently not associated with obsessive ideas. To be noted: actually, any psychic content can take an obsessive character (ideas, images, memories, fears, impulses).

Overvalued Idea

An overvalued idea is an ideational content with strong affective tone that dominates consciousness (and the person's life). It is not absurd and such as the subject can recognize the excessiveness (accessible to criticism).

The overvalued idea is strengthened usually based on a personality disorder and frequently leads to action. It resembles obsessive ideas for the pervasive dominance in thought; it differs for the remarkable emotional charge and the egosyntonic experience. That means that the subject experiences it as its own and not as intrusive (without suffering).

Personality Disorder

Class of mental illness characterized by enduring maladaptive patterns of behavior, cognition, and inner experience, exhibited across many contexts and deviating markedly from those accepted by the individual's culture. These patterns develop early, are inflexible, and are associated with significant distress or disability. (American Psychiatric Association, *DSM-5*, see bibliography)

Psychosis

Today the term has fallen into disuse. Just the adjective "psychotic" is still largely employed to define a severe psychiatric disorder, with detachment from reality and presence of "positive symptoms" such as delusions and hallucinations and "negative symptoms" such as unsociability, apathy, and attention impairments.

Schizophrenia

The term schizophrenia labels a set of clinical conditions characterized by chronic deterioration of personality, psychotic symptoms (delusions; catatonia, which is the dissociation between will and movement; and ideational disorders) at least at some stage of the course. Because the disorder has an early onset and a highly debilitating potential, though not frequent, it represents a high social cost and one of the largest commitments to psychiatric services, rehabilitation, and care. The concept of schizophrenia has undergone several revisions over time with large swings in the delimitation diagnostics and even radical criticisms that have questioned the very possibility of describing a well-defined clinical entity with this term.

Bibliography

American Psychiatric Association. *DSM-5*. Washington, DC: APA, 2013

Avenanti, A., et al. "Transcranial Magnetic Stimulation Highlights the Sensorimotor Side of Empathy for Pain." *Nature Neuroscience* 8 (2005): 955–960.

Brennan, J. H., and D. R. Hemsley. "Illusory Correlations in Paranoid and Non-Paranoid Schizophrenia." *British Journal of Clinical Psychology* 23 (1984): 225–226.

Canetti, E. *Masse und Macht* (translated *Crowds and Power*). Hamburg: Claassen, Verlag, 1960.

Cargnello, D. *Il caso Ernst Wagner.* Milano: Feltrinelli, 1984.

Cassano, G. B., et al. *Trattato Italiano di Psichiatria.* Milano: Masson, 1999.

Cioni, P., and E. Poli, edited by G. B. Cassano, A. Tundo. "Disturbi deliranti in" *Psicopatologia e Clinica Psichiatrica*, Torino: UTEBrat'jaT, 2007.

Damasio, A. *Looking for Spinoza: Joy, Sorrow, and the Feeling Brain.* Eugene: Harvest, 2003.

Davis, M. H. "Measuring Individual Differences in Empathy: Evidence for a Multidimensional Approach." *Journal of Personality and Social Psychology* 44 (1983): 113–236.

Davis, M. H. *Empathy. A Social Psychological Approach.* Madison: Brown and Benchmark, 1994.

Della Luna, M., and P Cioni. *Neuroschiavi*. Cesena: Macroedizioni, 2011.

Della Luna, M. *Le chiavi del potere*. Roma: Koiné, 2003.

Doidge, N. *The Brain That Changes Itself.* New York: Penguin Books, 2007.

Dostoyevskij, F. *The Brothers Karamazov.* Russian: *Brat'ja Karamazovi,* Moscow: The Russian Messenger, 1880.

Fenigstein, A. and P. A. Venable. "Paranoia and Self-consciousness." *Journal of Personality and Social Psychology* 62 (1992): 129–134.

Frith, C. *The Cognitive Neuropsychology of Schizophrenia.* Mahwaw: Lawrence Erlbaum Ltd., 1992.

Frith, C. *Making up the Mind: How the Brain Creates Our Mental World.* Oxford: Blackwell Ltd., 2007.

Goldie P. *The Emotions, A Philosophical Exploration,* Oxford: Clarendon Press, 2000.

Grove, W. M., & Barden, R. C. Protecting the integrity of the legal system: The admissibility of testimony from mental health experts under Daubert/Kumho analyses. Psychology, Public Policy, and Law, 5 (1999), 224–242.

Johnson, M. *The Meaning of the Body.* Chicago: The University of Chicago Press, 2007.

Hemsley, D. R. and P. A. Garety. "The Formation and Maintenance of Delusions: A Bayesian Analysis." *British Journal of Psychiatry* 149 (1986): 51–56.

Kraepelin, E. *Compendium of Psychiatry. 8th ed.* German: *Kompendium der Psychiatrie,* Leipzig: Abel, 1915.

Kutchera, K. *Quasiamore.* Barrafranca: Bonfirraro Editore, in press.

Lacan, J. *De la psychose paranoïaque dans ses rapports avec la personalité.* Paris: Le Français, 1932.

Lavoine, P. L. *Le malade mental dangereux.* Paris: Editions Hospitalières, 1998.

Legrenzi, P. and C. Umiltà. *Neuro-Mania.* Bologna: Il Mulino, 2009.

Lusetti, W. *Cannibalismo ed evoluzione.* Roma: Armando Editore, 2008.

Musil, R. *The Man Without Qualities.* German: *Der Mann ohne Eigenschaften.* Berlin: Rowohlt Verlag, 1930.

Poli, E. and P. Cioni. "Psicopatologia generale." *Manuale di Psichiatria,* edited by Cassano, Cioni, Perugi, Poli. Torino: UTET, 1994.

Raichle, M. E. et al. "A Default Mode of Brain Function." *Proc. Natl. Acad. Sci. USA* 98 (2001): 676–682.

Sacks, O. *Hallucinations.* New York: Vintage, 2013.

Scheier, M. F. and C. S. Carver. "The Self-Consciousness Scale: A Revised Version for Use with General Populations." *Journal of Applied Social Psychology* 15(8) (1985): 687–699.

Schreber, D. P. *Memorie di un malato di nervi,* ed. it. Milano: Adelphi, 1974.

Taylor. K. *Brainwashing.* Oxford: Oxford University Press, 2004.

Rear Cover

Paolo Cioni is an Italian psychiatrist (born near Pisa in 1951 and living in Florence) with long-term community, hospital, and academic experience.

He has been published with all the major Italian editors in the branch of psychiatry. Now practicing as a consultant in the clinical and forensic fields, he enjoys addressing themes of his own interest without being tied to the paradigms of the category. He began a new creative phase with the publication of *Neuroschiavi (Neuroslaves)* with Marco Della Luna (2009), as well as the French version, *Neuro-Esclaves* (second edition, 2013). He had good success in the presentation of his book in Paris (March 2014): more than twenty thousand hits of the videoconference on YouTube and twelve thousand for his interview on the subject of mental manipulations of all kinds.

He recently published *Paranoia tra Leadership e Fallimento* (*Paranoia Between Leadership and Failure*), one of his favorite themes, which expands paranoia from the individual psychiatric level to sociology and politics. The message is that paranoia is a dangerous condition. It is underestimated and contagious, especially in a world where the Internet dominates. Paranoid websites are expanding their influence every day while society is unable to defend itself.

At least one paranoiac might well live in your condo.

The book gives information about how to unmask paranoiacs, how to behave with them, and how to treat them, including some original and innovative suggestions.